THE STORY OF
NEW ZEALAND

~THE STORY OF~
NEW ZEALAND

Judith Bassett, Keith Sinclair
and Marcia Stenson

REED

Published by Reed Books, a division of Reed Publishing (NZ) Ltd, 39 Rawene Rd, Birkenhead, Auckland. Associated companies, branches and representatives throughout the world.

ISBN 0 7900 0644 8

Cover designed by Michele Stutton
Text designed by Sharon Grace

First published 1985
Reprinted 1987, 1990, 1992, 1993, 1995, 1996, 1997
New edition 1998
Reprinted 2000, 2002, 2004

Printed in Singapore by Kyodo Printing Co (S'pore) Pte Ltd

Contents

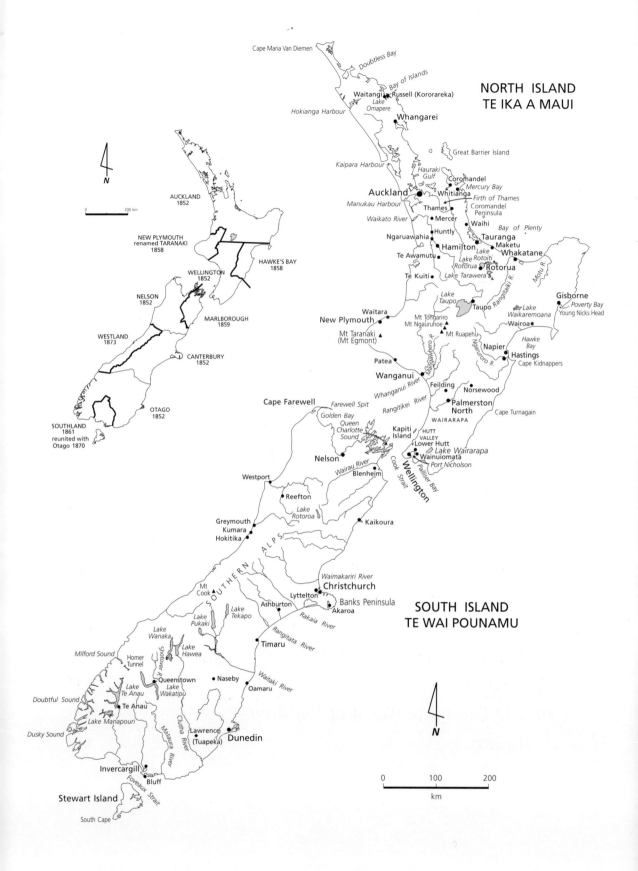

NORTH ISLAND
TE IKA A MAUI

Cape Maria Van Diemen
Doubtless Bay
Bay of Islands
Waitangi Russell (Kororareka)
Lake Omapere
Hokianga Harbour
Whangarei
Great Barrier Island
Kaipara Harbour
Hauraki Gulf
Coromandel
Mercury Bay
Auckland
Whitianga
Firth of Thames
Manukau Harbour
Thames
Coromandel Peninsula
Waikato River
Mercer
Waihi
Bay of Plenty
Huntly
Ngaruawahia
Tauranga
Maketu
Hamilton
Whakatane
Te Awamutu
Lake Rotoiti
Lake Rotorua
Rotorua
Te Kuiti
Lake Tarawera
Motu R.
Rangitaiki R.
Lake Taupo
Gisborne
Taupo
Lake Waikaremoana
Poverty Bay
Young Nicks Head
Waitara
Mt Tongariro
Wairoa
New Plymouth
Mt Ngauruhoe
Mt Ruapehu
Mt Taranaki (Mt Egmont)
Napier
Hawke Bay
Hastings
Cape Kidnappers
Patea
Wanganui
Feilding
Norsewood
Whanganui River
Rangitikei River
Palmerston North
Cape Turnagain
Cape Farewell
WAIRARAPA
Farewell Spit
Golden Bay
Kapiti Island
HUTT VALLEY
Queen Charlotte Sound
Lower Hutt
Lake Wairarapa
Nelson
Wainuiomata
Port Nicholson
Wairau River
Wellington
Palliser Bay
Blenheim
Cook Strait
Westport
Reefton
Lake Rotoroa
Greymouth
Kaikoura
Kumara
Hokitika
SOUTHERN ALPS
Waimakariri River
Christchurch
Mt Cook
Lyttelton
Banks Peninsula
Ashburton
Akaroa
Lake Tekapo
SOUTH ISLAND
TE WAI POUNAMU
Rakaia River
Lake Pukaki
Rangitata River
Lake Wanaka
Timaru
Milford Sound
Lake Hawea
Homer Tunnel
Waitaki River
Lake Te Anau
Queenstown
Naseby
Lake Wakatipu
Doubtful Sound
Oamaru
Te Anau
Clutha River
Lake Manapouri
Mataura River
Lawrence (Tuapeka)
Dusky Sound
Dunedin
Shotover River
Invercargill
Bluff
Foveaux Strait
Stewart Island
South Cape

AUCKLAND 1852
NEW PLYMOUTH renamed TARANAKI 1858
HAWKE'S BAY 1858
WELLINGTON 1852
NELSON 1852
MARLBOROUGH 1859
WESTLAND 1873
CANTERBURY 1852
OTAGO 1852
SOUTHLAND 1861 reunited with Otago 1870

N

0   200 km

0   100   200
km

N

Introduction

We wrote this book because we thought young people would like to read a history of New Zealand that was written specially for them. It needed to be a complete history — from the earliest times to our own time, and it needed to take into account the newest writing and work on New Zealand history. We begin the story with New Zealand's origins in Gondwanaland to help readers to understand that this land is distinct from others and that it is very old.

The history of a country is a story of people and the changes in their lives. When we began to write about the different kinds of people who have come to New Zealand we remembered that many were children. This is not a textbook. It is a book for children to read for themselves. They will find many people of their own ages in it. Some of these young people are completely new 'characters' in our history. They really lived and we have found out about them and written their stories for the first time.

Among the children who appear are the Maori hero, Maui, and 'Young Nick', one of the discoverers of New Zealand. Then there is young Te Taniwha, who saw Captain Cook, and James Caddell, the only survivor of a sealing gang. There is Christina McIlvride, who delivered the mails; Albert Blanch, who collected birds' eggs; and several others, such as 'Dodge' Brown, who drove a car to school in the twenties.

There are several other books available for children which have stories about New Zealand or which describe pieces of our history. This book is an introduction to the main patterns and the main themes of our nation's growth. We have also written it with the new social history in mind. As well as the Governors, chiefs and Prime Ministers of New Zealand, there are plenty of ordinary people. We have paid special attention to the kinds of lives lived by women and children: how they earned their living, what they did in their spare time.

The authors have written several kinds of books before — history books, biographies, poetry, textbooks and children's stories. But this one is a new kind of book for them. None of us has written a history book for — and about — young people before. We would like to thank our friends — both adults and children — who have read some of the chapters and also the librarians at the Alexander Turnbull Library and the Auckland Institute, who have helped to find material for the book. They include Erik Olssen, Judith Binney, Jamie Belich, Bruce Biggs, Claudia Orange, Gordon Maitland, and Joan McCracken.

Judith Bassett
Keith Sinclair
Marcia Stenson

ONE

A Land of Birds

About two hundred million years ago New Zealand was part of the shore of a southern continent that lay near the South Pole, which has been given the name Gondwanaland. Over a vast period of time it broke up into South America, Africa, India, Australia, Antarctica and New Zealand. The different parts slowly drifted apart. This is called 'continental drift'.

New Zealand finished up in a position extremely isolated from other lands — about 1,600 kilometres from Australia, 1,700 kilometres from Tonga, and 2,300 kilometres from Antarctica.

This history of our country's geology — that is, the story of the land itself — had many important results. One was that some ancient species were preserved. Because the country was so isolated they were protected from enemies that would have killed them. These survivals from very early times include the tuatara (a lizard-like reptile) and the New Zealand native frogs.

Fossils of dinosaurs who roamed in Hawke's Bay 65 million years ago have been found, but the islands had moved away from the body of Gondwanaland before the appearance of mammals, or even of the primitive mammals, the marsupials, like the kangaroos, which reached Australia. The bats were New Zealand's only land mammals and they probably flew in later, though they, too, were very ancient species.

The forests of New Zealand include some direct descendants of those of Gondwanaland, for instance the kauri, the kahikatea and the rimu. The New Zealand trees are very old. By contrast, the plants and animals of the Northern

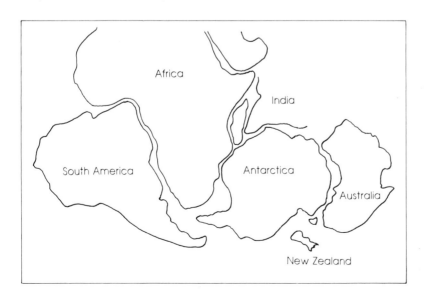

The continent of Gondwanaland broke up like a jigsaw puzzle into smaller land masses.

Opposite page:
New Zealand forest.

Hemisphere are relatively young. Their ancestors were wiped out by an ice age, fifty thousand years ago. Some of the New Zealand trees themselves, like the largest kauri, are believed to be up to two thousand years old, which puts them among the oldest living things on earth.

Another result of distance was that it was very hard for plants, animals or people to get to New Zealand. Some seeds were washed ashore, or carried by sea birds in their stomachs. But the plants, in general, evolved into very distinctive forms over long periods of time. Most of the plants in New Zealand were not to be found growing anywhere else.

Birds flew in too, or were blown in by storms, particularly from across the Tasman Sea. They still do, like the white eye (or silver eye) last century or the white-faced heron and the welcome swallow more recently.

Of course, New Zealand had a very vigorous insect life within the plant world. But the land was ruled by birds. The grasslands and the forests were grazed — not by kangaroos or bison or buffalo — but by birds. The biggest, the flightless giant moa, stood three metres high. There were smaller flightless birds like the kiwi. They, too, are believed to descend from flightless birds of Gondwanaland. The absence of mammals or of other enemies helps to explain why flightless birds could survive and thrive in New Zealand.

According to an early Maori legend, when the first Polynesian explorer, Kupe, landed in Aotearoa he was greeted by only two 'beings', kokako and piwakawaka. Certainly the most obvious thing the first humans to arrive in New Zealand noticed was that it was occupied mainly by birds.

TWO

~

The Maori People

One result of the distance between New Zealand and other lands was that it was one of the last countries of any size to be populated by human beings. The first people to reach New Zealand were Polynesians. They were a people originating in Asia, who entered the western Pacific about four thousand years ago. It is not known when they came to New Zealand, but probably it was over a thousand years ago. The Polynesians were great sailors and explorers. They often made long sea voyages out of sight of land. Sometimes they were lost and discovered new islands by accident. Sometimes they decided to set out in search of new homes.

These canoes, racing in 1903, look little different from those seen by Captain Cook.

The myth of Maui

A widespread Polynesian story describes the feats of a mythical ancestor, Maui, who fished up islands. Maui was a mischievous boy and a magician who played tricks on his parents. Once he turned himself into a pigeon and sat in a tree throwing berries at them.

Maui thought that Ra, the sun, moved too fast, so he and his brothers snared him and beat him with the jaw-bone of his grandmother, Murirangawhenua, until, bruised and sore, Ra had to crawl slowly across the sky forever.

One day, so a Maori legend says, Maui went out fishing with his brothers. He induced them to sail far to the south in unknown waters. When he decided to try his luck he used his grandmother's jaw-bone for a hook. He hit himself on the nose and used his blood for bait. With this magical hook and charmed bait he caught a monstrous fish, the North Island of New Zealand, which the Maori called Te Ika a Maui (the Fish of Maui). The South Island was Maui's canoe and Stewart Island its anchor stone.

The arrival of the Maori

According to some Maori, their ancestors came to New Zealand in a fleet of canoes, the names of which, like Tainui and Te Arawa, are remembered in different areas of the country. The 'fleet' is a legend, not a fact, but it is true that the Polynesians came in canoes. Possibly only one canoe crossed the stormy and desolate seas to reach what the Maori came to call Aotearoa. It is thought that this meant Land of the Long Daylight. In the tropics there is no twilight and Polynesian people would have found this surprising when they reached New Zealand. One canoe load would have been enough to produce the Maori population of perhaps one hundred thousand, which the Europeans met a thousand years later. The Polynesians came from a place they called Hawaiki, in eastern Polynesia, perhaps the Cook Islands, Tahiti or the Marquesas Islands. No one knows for sure.

The Polynesians brought with them the rat and dog, but they left behind — or perhaps lost overboard or ate — the pig and the domestic fowl, which they called the moa. They brought some food plants, including kumara, taro, the gourd and yam. The fact that they brought with them several animals and food plants strongly suggests that they were not a fishing party which was lost; rather that they set out on a voyage in search of new islands.

A great deal is known about the first New Zealanders from the study by scientists of their skeletons and teeth, and the sites they occupied. In the early centuries of settlement they had an extremely good diet — plenty of seals and kumara and birds, especially the giant moa, which weighed up to 240 kilos. It must have been an easy prey to daring and hungry men. Certainly the Polynesians helped to kill off the moa, and the seals in the north. The teeth from early Maori graves are often perfect, indicating an abundance of good and soft food.

Later, by about the fifteenth century, the climate had become cooler and the population had increased. Food had become scarcer. No doubt there were plenty of fish to be caught on the coast. But people were eating more shellfish, especially pipi (which generally contain sand), and chewing fern root, which, like sand, harshly wore down the teeth. People's teeth were often worn down to the gum by the time they were in their mid-twenties. Life was hard.

After the Europeans arrived, bringing the potato, which could be grown everywhere in New Zealand, Maori teeth again became perfect.

The average size of Maori was much bigger than that of Europeans at that time. Two hundred years ago the height of European men averaged about 160 centimetres; Maori men were about 175 centimetres tall on average. Like other 'pre-

historic' people, however, they did not live very long. Carrying heavy loads, like tree trunks and canoes, damaged their spines. They had little knowledge of medicine. They believed that illness was caused by makutu (witchcraft), or from infringing tapu (doing things that were forbidden).

Although the early Maori suffered from few diseases, like most ancient people they could expect to live only about thirty years. Few lived into their forties or later. The idea that the life expectancy of most people is 'three-score years and ten' has only recently been true. For most people, in most centuries before ours, it was much less than that.

Dr Peter Buck (later Sir Peter Buck), whose Maori name was Te Rangi Hiroa, and two friends pretending to hunt a stuffed moa. Sir Peter Buck became a famous anthropologist (a person who studies mankind).

The lifestyle of the early Maori

Perhaps the greatest achievement of the New Zealand Polynesians was to learn to adapt a tropical lifestyle to a temperate land. One example is that in the tropics the kumara is a perennial plant, highly susceptible to frosts. In their new land the people discovered that they could store the kumara tubers in pits in the earth and then plant out the shoots in the next spring. But, of course, in a colder climate, clothing and houses and many other aspects of life had to be changed.

The Polynesian settlers brought the paper mulberry plant with them to make tapa cloth, but it grew only in the north. They had to learn how to plait cloth out of New Zealand flax. They also made rain capes from flax, sometimes covered with feathers, or with strips of dog-skin.

The Maori lived in quite small whare (houses), which must have been very smoky when winter fires were burning. It seems that there were few, if any, of the large, elaborately carved and decorated meeting houses that were built after the Europeans came.

The houses were grouped in kainga (villages), and in some districts these were situated near a pa. Here food was stored and the people could retreat to these fortified hilltops if threatened by an enemy. The hills in the modern city of Auckland still reveal the terraced defences dug by people of past centuries.

Warfare, often for utu (revenge or payment), was a frequent feature of the life of the Maori, as it was of contemporary European people like the English and Scots. Danger was a daily hazard. The Maori warrior, like the English soldier, sought honour and fame in the assault with the patu (club) as in the cannon's mouth. Boys expected to grow up to be warriors.

Dangers were not only from war, any more than they are for us today. Since the Maori were seafarers and river travellers, drowning was a constant risk. Even as late as the nineteenth century the most common cause of accidental death was drowning. This danger is recalled in a Maori legend about a canoe in the ancestral home, Hawaiki. When great waves began to pour over a canoe, a girl named

The Maori terraces on One Tree Hill. Its Maori name is Maungakiekie (mountain of the kiekie — an edible plant). It was a huge pa.

Wairaka had to take over. She called out, 'I will take the part of the man!' When her descendants reached New Zealand they remembered her heroic feat. The word 'tane' means man; 'Whakatane' means to act the role of a man.

The Maori had not invented writing, but much of their history is recorded in the names of places. For instance, on the Coromandel peninsula there is a beach called Kikowhakarere, which means 'the flesh thrown away' or 'left behind'. This is said to record a cannibal feast suddenly interrupted by an enemy attack. Sometimes the Maori were cannibals, a fact that upset the first European explorers.

Most Maori knowledge was handed on in speech — for instance, knowledge about fish and birds and plants. Knowledge of the ancestors was learned by heart in the tribal whakapapa (genealogies, or lists of ancestors).

Yet life was not always violent. There was an elaborate network of tribal alliances and friendships. There was no trade for money, but there was a wide-spread system of exchanging gifts. Muttonbirds and greenstone from the South Island, which the Maori called Te Wai Pounamu (the Water of Jade), and obsidian, a volcanic glass found in a few places and used to make knives and other sharp tools, were widely distributed throughout the country through exchanges between the tribes. They were also prizes of war.

Nowhere in the Pacific, between Peru and Indonesia, were metals known to man. Maori ornaments, like the tiki, and their weapons were made of stone. So were their tools, such as the adze and the axe. Thousands of stone and bone implements or pendants may be seen in museums. They take us back, in our imagination, to those earlier times.

Early Maori society

Like many other people, for instance the Scottish clans, Maori felt an intense closeness to their kin. They lived within the whanau and then within their extended family, cousins and other relations, called the hapu. The largest group they called iwi. They did not think of themselves as one people. They belonged to their tribes.

The tribes were ruled by the rangatira. The ordinary people were called tutua. Some of the great chiefs like Te Wherowhero, a Waikato chief, were famous throughout the land. He was (as we shall see) to become the first Maori King, taking the name Potatau. Some women were also chiefs. One was a poet, Tope-ora, who was a sister of Te Rauparaha, a noted chief himself. She was later to be one of the few women who signed the Treaty of Waitangi.

A famous chief was said to have great mana, which meant prestige and power. He was tapu (sacred). Tapu is an idea central to Maori life. The kumara gardens were tapu. So were certain places. The birth of a child was tapu. Anyone who offended against tapu was in great danger of punishment by the gods. The Maori believed that there were many gods — not all of them friendly.

The life of Maori children

Life in early Maori society was perhaps more dangerous for children than it is today, in the sense that an enemy attack was always possible. But in their family they enjoyed aroha as much as in any other family. Sometimes they had to work hard, gathering pipi or snaring birds or collecting edible plants, such as puha.

Children were taught the traditions and names of their ancestors and all sorts of useful information by the tribal elders (kaumatua) and sometimes by a tohunga (priest). Some tribes had a whare wananga (house of learning).

Most Maori games were like those still played today. For instance, the Maori had a game played with five pebbles almost the same as the English knuckle-bones. They had darts, stilts, spinning tops, puppets and kites. They played at skipping and on swings. Some of these games, like stick games, aimed at improving agility and swiftness of the eye, which would be useful to a warrior in battle. Wrestling was the most highly regarded of athletic exercises. Boys were also taught to practise war dances and the use of weapons such as the patu and the taiaha. Girls learned to gather and preserve food and some were taught difficult skills such as weaving fine cloaks.

THREE

~

The Explorers

Europeans in the seventeenth and early eighteenth centuries knew very little about the Southern Hemisphere. Of New Zealand they knew nothing at all. The first European explorers to visit the South Pacific were looking for a great land said to exist in the south. Geographers felt sure that there must be a large landmass in the south, a great southern continent, to balance the northern continents. The explorers were to prove that this theory was wrong.

Abel Tasman

Abel Janszoon Tasman was sent by the Governor-General of Batavia, the Dutch trading post in Java, to find this southern continent and to establish trade there. Dutch captains had already mapped part of the Australian coast, but there was nothing known to Europeans about what lay further east.

Abel Tasman was given two ships for this task, the flagship *Heemskerck*, armed for fighting, and the *Zeehaen*, a long, narrow, shallow-draughted, fast ship. He had goods for trade. On the *Heemskerck*, as well as cloth he had:

10 Golconda blankets
500 Chinese small mirrors
90 kilograms of ironmongery
Quantities of cloves, mace, nutmegs and pewter
50 Chinese gold wire
10 packets of Chinese gold wire
25 pieces of assorted iron pots
3 pearls and a large brass basin.

Tasman sailed from Batavia via Mauritius in 1642. His instructions were to treat any 'savages' with caution but kindness. He landed briefly on Tasmania, where footholds on a tree nearly two metres apart and ghostly voices in the bush led his crew to call it the Land of Giants. After another seven days' sailing they sighted the west coast of the South Island. A rough sea made

Abel Tasman, the first known European explorer to see New Zealand.

A. Zijn onze Schepen
B. Zijn de prauwen die om ons boort quamen
C. is des Zeehaens prauken dat na ons boort quam schipper van ... des landts vermeestert en dat nae schieten widerom ... heeft door wij Zagen dat 2 Prauwen Volaget hadden is onse schuijt met onse Sch... widerom gehaelt
D. is 't de Vsthooningh van hare prauwen in het fatzon ...
E. Zijn onze Schepen die onder Zeijle gatn
F. is onze schaloup die de Prauwen widerom ... hadde

Aldus Vsthoont de Moordenaers Baij als wij op 15 Vademen daer in geanckert leght

'A View of Murderers' Bay (when anchored at 15 fathoms).' An illustration from Tasman's journal. In the foreground is the Maori war party, in a double canoe, with the leader standing. In the background the artist shows the incident that led to the bay being called Murderers' Bay. The ship's boat was rammed by the canoes, and the Dutchmen were struck by short thick pieces of wood. Three were killed and one died later of his wounds.

landing impossible, so they sailed north to anchor in the sheltered waters of Tasman Bay. Here they hoped to establish friendly relations with the Maori. However, before Tasman even had a chance to land, warriors from the Ngati Tumata Kokiri tribe attacked one of his small boats and killed four of his crew. Tasman took fright, weighed anchor and sailed off. He called the area Murderers' Bay. It is now called Golden Bay.

He tried to sail east between the North Island and the South Island but his high-built ships could not make headway against the strong currents and contrary winds. He then sailed north up the west coast of the North Island, naming the northern cape after the wife of his Governor-General, Maria van Diemen. He made another attempt to land on the far northern Three Kings Islands but was once again driven off by Maori. Tasman called the land he had found Staten Landt, but after a few years it became known in Holland, and then in Europe, as Novo Zeelandia (New Zeeland). Zeeland is a coastal province in Holland.

Tasman's journal and his incomplete chart of the coast of New Zealand became well known to other explorers. However, his reports of the new land did not sound attractive to traders, and it was many years before the next European explorer was seen off the coast.

James Cook

On 6 October 1769 a small boy called
Nicholas Young was at the masthead of a
British ship called the *Endeavour*. His captain, James Cook, had promised a reward to
the first person to sight land. They had been
at sea for some weeks on a voyage of scientific exploration of the South Pacific.
They had spent some time in Tahiti, observ-
ing the transit of Venus across the face of
the sun. By comparing observations taken
at different points of the earth's surface, scientists hoped to be able to work out the distance between the earth and the sun. Now
they were fulfilling the second part of their
instructions — to learn more of the land
reported by Abel Tasman. Their task was to
find out if it was indeed the great southern
continent geographers had talked of.

At 2 p.m. Nicholas Young shouted 'Land!' and became the first
European to see the east coast of the North Island. A gallon of rum
was the reward Cook promised. Whether Nick Young received
the rum we do not know, but as Cook had also promised, the land
he sighted was named after him — Young Nick's Head. Next day,
James Cook anchored the *Endeavour* in a bay near the mouth of
a small river, the site of modern Gisborne. They could see a Maori
settlement ashore and Cook hoped to make contact with them. To
Cook's surprise and confusion, the Maori response was proud and
aggressive. They saw these intruders as a threat and determined
to drive them off. In self-defence the crew of the *Endeavour*
killed a number of the Maori and Cook left the area he called
Poverty Bay, much distressed by his failure.

Further south they tried again. On board was a young boy called
Taiata, from the islands in the Tahiti group. He was the servant of
a chief, Tupaea, who sailed with Cook as guide and interpreter.
Taiata was leaning over the side of the ship while Cook was trying
to barter some cloth for dried fish. Suddenly the boy was grabbed

*Nicholas Young's
commanding officer,
Lieutenant James Cook,
had been promoted to
captain by the time that
this portrait was painted.
Cook had won a good
reputation as a naval
surveyor and careful
scientific observer and
was asked to take
command of the
expedition.*

*Young Nick's Head. Drawn
by Sydney Parkinson, the
artist on board the
Endeavour.*

View of the North Side of the Entrance into Poverty Bay, & Morai Island, in New-Zealand.

A Maori chief drawn by Sydney Parkinson during the exploration of New Zealand by the Endeavour. *Cook invited the warriors on board his ship.*

by the Maori and carried off in their canoe. Cook ordered his marines to open fire and several of the kidnappers were killed. In the confusion Taiata was able to leap into the sea and swim back to the *Endeavour*, where a boat was quickly lowered to pick him up. Cook named the area Cape Kidnappers after the incident.

Maori reaction to Europeans

Cook explored the east coast of New Zealand, sailing south as far as Cape Turnagain. Friendly contact with the Maori tribes was established. Cook received fresh supplies and in return traded beads, Tahitian cloth, nails and axes. At Mercury Bay, off Whitianga, Cook spent eleven days. Many years later, a famous chief, Te Horeta Taniwha, who had been a small boy at the time, described what he remembered of this visit:

> In the days long past, when I was a very little boy, a vessel came to Whitianga. . .
> .when our old men saw the ship they said it was a tupua, a god, and the people on

board were strange beings. The ship came to anchor, and the boats pulled on shore. As our old men looked at the manner in which they came on shore, the rowers pulling with their backs to the bows of the boat, the old people said, 'Yes, it is so: these people are goblins; their eyes are at the back of their heads; they pull on shore with their backs to the land to which they are going.'

At first the women and children ran to hide in the forest, but when they saw that their warriors were not harmed, they came out of hiding.

These goblins began to gather oysters, and we gave some kumara, fish, and fern-root to them. These they accepted, and we [the women and children] began to roast cockles for them; and as we saw that these goblins were eating kumara, fish, and cockles, we were startled, and said, 'Perhaps they are not goblins like the Maori goblins.

'Te Taniwha or Hook Nose.' A sketch of Te Horeta Taniwha, when he was very old. He met Cook at Mercury Bay in November 1769. This sketch was made in 1853.

These 'goblins' had some strange habits.

Now some of the goblins had walking-sticks which they carried about with them, and when we arrived at the bare dead trees where the shags roost at night and have their nests, the goblins lifted the walking-sticks up and pointed them at the birds, and in a short time thunder was heard to crash and a flash of lightning was seen, and a shag fell from the trees; and we children were terrified, and fled, and rushed into the forest, and left the goblins all alone.

Cook's men persuaded Te Horeta Taniwha and his friends to come back and look at the dead bird, but they were most bewildered by what had happened. How had the bird been killed?

We were now at quiet and peace with them, and they gave us some of the food they had brought on shore with them. Some of this food was very hard, but it was sweet. Some of our old people said it was punga-punga [pumice stone — in fact it was ship's biscuit] from the land from which these goblins came. They gave us some fat food [dried beef], which the same old people of our tribe said was the flesh of whales; but the saltness of this food nipped our throats, and we did not care for such fat food.

Cook invited some of the warriors on board his ship. A few brave boys including Te Horeta Taniwha went with the warriors.

We sat on the deck of the ship, where we were looked at by the goblins, who with their hands stroked our mats and the hair of the heads of us children; at the same time they made much gabbling noise in talking, which we thought was questions

regarding our mats and the sharks' teeth we wore in our ears, and the
hei-tiki we wore suspended on our chests; but as we could not understand them we laughed, and they laughed also.

He was given a present by Cook himself.

> I and my two boy companions did not walk about on board of the ship — we were
> afraid lest we should be bewitched by the goblins; and we sat still and looked at
> everything we saw at the home of these goblins. When the chief goblin had been
> away in that part of their ship which he occupied, he came up on deck again and
> came to where I and my two boy companions were, and patted our heads with his
> hand, and he put his hand out towards me and spoke to us at the same time, hold-
> ing a nail out towards us. My companions were afraid, and sat in silence; but I
> laughed, and he gave the nail to me. I took it into my hand and said 'Ka Pai' ['it's
> good'], and he repeated my words, and again patted our heads with his hand, and
> went away.

The present was very valuable and Te Horeta Taniwha treasured it dearly.

> I took my nail, and kept it with great care, and carried it with me wherever I went,
> and made it fit to the point of my spear, and also used it to make holes in the side-
> boards of canoes, to bind them on to the canoe. I kept this nail till one day I was
> in a canoe and she capsized in the sea, and my god was lost to me.

Circumnavigating New Zealand

Cook sailed around North Cape, passing without realising it a French ship, the
Saint Jean Baptiste. He followed the coastline down the west of the North
Island and anchored in Queen Charlotte Sound, where he spent three weeks
working on his ship, trading with the local Maori for supplies and collecting

Plate XXV

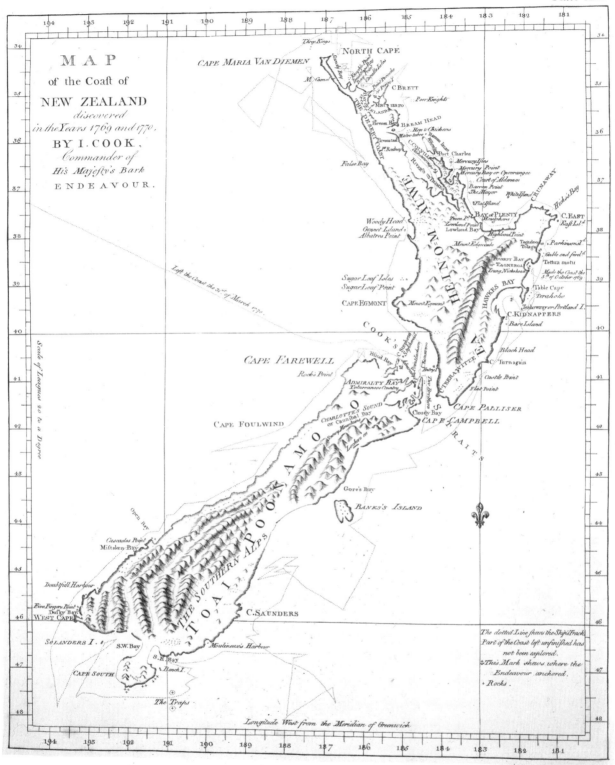

James Cook's chart of New Zealand was surprisingly accurate in spite of the problems of navigating in unknown waters. Notice that Banks Peninsula, Foveaux Strait and the Hauraki Gulf are not accurate.

fresh food. He sailed through the strait now called Cook Strait and up to Cape Turnagain to prove to his officers that the North Island was in fact an island. He then turned south to circumnavigate the South Island.

Cook carefully plotted the coastline, made good maps of the two main islands and kept excellent records of all his dealings with the Maori tribes. He made a few serious errors on his charts, some of which he himself corrected on later voyages. It was not easy to navigate on an unknown coast, sometimes in bad weather.

Aboard the *Endeavour* was Joseph Banks, a wealthy gentleman whose interest in botany had brought him on this long voyage. He collected and catalogued the new plants, birds and insects previously unknown to Europe. While Banks collected, his artist Sydney Parkinson sketched scenes from the new land. Banks was disappointed that Cook thought it was too dangerous to sail into Doubtful Sound; he was sure that many new plants were to be found there. After six to seven months tracing the coastline of New Zealand, Cook finally set sail for Australia.

The French ship that he had unknowingly passed in the north was commanded by Jean-François Marie de Surville, who was on a voyage of trade and treasure-seeking. His men were very ill; sixty had died, and the survivors were weak from scurvy. He anchored in Doubtless Bay, north of the Bay of Islands. After difficult weather and a violent clash with a Maori tribe, de Surville took to sea again, doing no more than making a chart of the Doubtless Bay area.

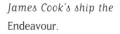

James Cook's ship the Endeavour.

James Cook returned to New Zealand again in 1773 and in 1777. He found that anchorages in Dusky Sound and Queen Charlotte Sound were useful places to rest, to re-supply the ship with fresh foods and to make repairs. On all his trips he tried to introduce new crops and animals. Potatoes and pigs were especially successful.

Relationships between the European explorers and the Maori tribes were often uneasy. Both were keen to trade. The explorers desperately needed fresh food and water after their long sea voyages. Maori soon learned the value of the axes, nails and cloth the Europeans offered in exchange. But neither people understood the other. Petty incidents some-times blew up into major confrontations. The French explorer Marion du Fresne, for example, with two officers and thirteen of his crew, was killed and eaten by Maori in the Bay of Islands in 1772. The remainder of his crew took fearful revenge, burning villages and canoes and butchering nearly 300 Maori. Both sides were bloodthirsty. The Europeans were often overconfident, sometimes carelessly infringing tapu and deeply offending their Maori hosts.

The difficulties in sailing a vessel on an uncharted shore are shown in this picture of the French ship the Astrolabe. *During her voyage off the coast of New Zealand she struck the rocks in a dangerous passage now called French Pass, between D'Urville Island and Tasman Bay. Luckily, she lifted off the rocks with only minor damage to her keel. Her captain, D'Urville, on this voyage in 1826-29 was able to improve Cook's chart.*

The reaction of the explorers

Portrait of a Maori chief by Parkinson. Cook described the Maori as strong, warlike people, brave and friendly.

What did they think of this new land which they had found? Tasman wrote in his log of 'a large land, uplifted high'. The sight of the Southern Alps to someone used to the lowlands of Batavia or the plains of Holland must have been awe-inspiring.

Cook's journal is full of admiration for the timber and the fertility of the soil. It was a land full of promise, a kind land where settlers from Europe could build a comfortable life. The local inhabitants were described most favourably. After a bad beginning, Cook had got on well with Maori. He described them as a strong, well-made people, active and warlike but not treacherous; a people who were both artistic and brave. They did not have a king or central government. Their prosperity varied from the comfortable circumstances of the tribes of the Bay of Islands to the apparent poverty of those present in Dusky Sound in the far south. Often Cook did not realise that he was meeting a tribe in a seasonal food-gathering place, rather than their main home area.

When James Cook's journals were published they were read widely in Europe. Explorers were much admired for their skill and courage, and James Cook became one of the most famous. People were eager to read about distant lands. They were very interested in learning more about how other people lived. Philosophers or thinkers of that time had put forward the theory that 'savage' men and women were happier than 'civilised' men and women. They felt that in a society where men and women had not learnt to use metals, and had not developed the modern sciences, their lives were more in tune with their surroundings. They pointed out that such men and women could swim better, run better, and see much further without a telescope than Europeans. A few Polynesians, like Omai from Tahiti, returned to Europe with the explorers. They were much admired, introduced into the best society and given many presents to take home. By the late eighteenth century these visitors and the wide publication of Cook's journals had brought the lands of the Pacific to the attention of Europeans.

FOUR

∽

Traders and Settlers

The first European traders, like the explorers, were not interested in living permanently in New Zealand. They wanted to make profits from the sale of natural resources like flax, timber, sealskins or whale oil. These products fetched good prices in Europe.

Sealers and whalers

From 1790 onwards ships from Sydney, Hobart, North America and Britain landed groups of men on the southern coast of the South Island and on the outlying islands to collect sealskins. These men were marooned for months and sometimes years at a time. They had very little shelter and only the bare essentials for food. The seal hunters were often escaped convicts and ruffians, and their leaders treated them very harshly. Discipline was very tough and men were often flogged. However, the seals were plentiful in number and easy to kill. Sometimes one sealing gang could collect 14,000 first-class skins in a season. The skins were sold to China, America and England to be made into fashionable felt hats. But by 1810 the fashions had changed and the sealskin trade was no longer profitable. Even though there was a brief revival in the 1820s and 1830s, the earlier

This sketch of a seal-hunt shows how easy it was to kill the seals.

Temporary camps were used by sealers while they collected the skins.

Below: Whaling could be very dangerous. Whaling ships like these called into New Zealand ports such as Kororareka to pick up fresh water and supplies.

hunters had killed too many of the seals for the trade to be important again.

Other visitors to New Zealand harbours were the deep-sea whalers, who hunted the cachalot or sperm whale. The oil from the whales was used in Europe for lubrication and lighting. High-quality candles were made from the spermacetic wax. Ambergris, a waxy material from the intestines of the sperm whale, was used in perfumes. The whaling ships called in for provisions and fresh water and to give crews a break from the long months at sea. Sometimes they needed replacement crews and several Maori served on whalers and travelled the world.

After 1820 bay whaling developed. From a base on shore, whalers would put out to sea in strong, well-built whale boats to hunt the black or right whale for its oil and bone. The whalebone was used for women's corsets, for umbrella ribs

and upholstery packing. From May to October, when the female whales came inshore to give birth, the whalers would kill the young calf and so trap the mother, who would refuse to leave her calf. During the remainder of the year the whalers would keep a small farm going or collect flax to trade with boats from Australia. Sometimes there would be more than a hundred men in about eighty cottages in these whaling stations. During the killing season the work was long and hard, but in the off-season the whalers were well known for their heavy drinking sessions. Many whalers were known by their nicknames, such as 'Flash Bill', 'Fat Jackson' or 'Black Peter'. The whaling stations were small villages, with the whalers' Maori wives working and gossiping, children playing, and dogs, pigs, goats and fowl running about.

The whale has been beached ready to be stripped of its blubber. The blubber was boiled down in trypots to produce whale oil.

Most of these whaling stations were in the South Island. Johnny Jones owned several in Otago and Southland. Dicky Barrett owned one of the few North Island stations, near New Plymouth. Not much money was needed to set up a shore-based whaling station. The only equipment necessary, apart from the boats, were trypots in which to boil the blubber, windlasses, knives and barrels. A small station could still make a profit with only three kills in a season. However, like the sealers before them, the whalers destroyed their own means of livelihood. Whales disappeared from the coast. At the same time vegetable oil began to replace whale oil. With less need for whale oil, people found better ways to invest their money. By the 1850s most of the whaling stations had disappeared from the coast.

The flax and timber trades

New Zealand flax was in great demand for ropes and cordage. The fibre prepared by Maori women, who scraped away the fleshy part with the sharp edge of a mussel shell, was of very high quality and attracted a good price. Traders and investors were very interested in New Zealand flax. The vast swamps with their acres and acres of flax seemed to promise future wealth. From 1815 to 1831 ships arrived frequently to collect a cargo of flax. Traders such as Philip Tapsell at Maketu in the Bay of Plenty exchanged muskets with the Arawa tribe for flax. One ton of fibre was worth one or two muskets.

However, it proved impossible to produce enough fibre in the traditional Maori way to meet the demand. All efforts to develop a technique to scrape the flax in huge quantities failed. Manila fibre from the Philippines proved to be more suitable for making ropes. After 1831 the trade in flax declined.

Flax was collected to make ropes and cords. It was, however, very difficult to prepare the fibre in large enough amounts to satisfy the demand.

The British navy was particularly interested in the high-quality timber of the New Zealand coasts. The kauri and kahikatea provided long, straight spars for masts and booms of sailing ships. The trees had to be growing close to the rivers or harbours to make transportation easy. The Hokianga harbour and the Thames coast were frequently visited by vessels looking for cargoes of spars. Kauri timber was particularly good for shipbuilding, whereas Maori builders had traditionally preferred the totara for canoes or buildings. Sawmills were soon established on the upper reaches of the Hokianga harbour to provide sawn timber for export.

The New Zealand kauri was in great demand for spars and shipbuilding. These paintings by Charles Heaphy show trees being sawn into logs (far right) and loaded aboard ship at Kohukohu on the Hokianga harbour.

31

Traders and the Maori

All these traders needed food and fresh water, as well as the flax or timber they

A sketch by Augustus Earle of Awow, the Maori wife of a European trader. Many traders found it useful to marry into the tribe with whom they lived.

were trading in. Maori bartered potatoes and pork for the goods they wanted from the strangers they called Pakeha. Cook had planted potatoes and Maori had quickly learned to cultivate them. Potatoes gave a bigger yield than kumara and were less trouble to grow. They also grew in areas too cold for the kumara. Pigs, too, had increased rapidly, and were a popular product to barter with European traders. Traders were also interested in Maori artefacts like mats, wooden carvings and, above all, shrunken tattooed human heads.

In exchange, Maori wanted nails, axes, muskets, blankets — the products they could not make themselves. A Russian visitor to Queen Charlotte Sound in 1820, Thaddeus Bellinghausen, describes the attitude of a chief to the gift of an axe:

I invited the chief into our cabin to dine with us. We seated him in the place of honour between Mr Lazarev and myself. He picked up and examined with astonishment, all the table utensils, but would not make use of them to eat with until someone gave him an example; then, carefully, but awkwardly, he put food in his mouth with a fork. The wine he drank without relish. Whilst at table, we continued to assure one another of mutual friendship by various signs and means of those few native words that I knew. But when later, wishing to give him more convincing proof of my good-will, I made him a present of a beautiful, well-polished axe, he jumped up from the table for joy and rushed up to the deck, whither I accompanied him. From there, he rushed towards his countrymen and, having embraced me, joyfully repeated 'Toki! Toki!' ['Axe! Axe!'].

The article that was in most demand was, however, the musket. Twenty-five bags of potatoes would buy a musket. At first Maori warriors had scoffed at the musket, thinking that it was a cowardly way to fight. They preferred the traditional hand-to-hand combat. It soon became clear, however, that a tribe with muskets had a great advantage. Hongi Hika, the Ngapuhi chief, demonstrated this very clearly. In 1820 he sailed to England on the ship *New Zealander* with the missionary Thomas Kendall. There, he helped scholars put together a Maori dictionary. Hongi Hika was very popular in England and gifts were showered on him. He was presented to King George IV at court and given a suit of chain mail. Before Hongi Hika returned to New Zealand he sold his presents and bought 300 muskets, though he kept the suit of chain mail. Once home again, he began a campaign against his old enemies, first in the Thames area and then in the Waikato. Their defeat by Hongi Hika and the loss of so many of their best warriors showed the Waikato tribes that to survive, they must have muskets.

One of the best ways to get muskets was to have your own Pakeha-Maori living with the tribe. These were European traders who collected flax or other articles of trade in return for muskets, blankets, axes and clothes. They usually operated on behalf of an agent or employer in Australia, and even though some married into the tribe and settled permanently, like Philip Tapsell, most returned to Australia after a few years. Some, like Barnet Burns, had tattooed faces, showing that they had become members of the tribe with whom they had lived. Here he describes why he had allowed himself to be tattooed:

> In the first place, I could travel to any part of the country, amongst my friends, if I thought proper. I was made and considered chief of a tribe of upwards of six hundred persons, consisting of men, women, and children. I could purchase flax when others could not. In fact, I was as well liked amongst the rest of the chiefs, as though I had been their brother.

Early European settlements

The two places that displayed the most permanent features of European settlement at this time were Kororareka, in the Bay of Islands, and the Hokianga harbour.

Kororareka (which means sweet penguin) was a supply post for the whalers, sealers and traders. It was like a shanty town, with few permanent buildings but often up to thirty ships anchored in the bay. The Bay of Islands provided excellent shelter for ships; there was plenty of fresh water close at hand and the Maori tribes had potatoes and pork to trade with the sailors. Maori farming impressed many traders. Crops included barley, maize, oats and wheat. Some of the surplus was sent to New South Wales. Less attractive was the trade in girls and the drunkenness and violence for which Kororareka became notorious.

In 1838 the town's inhabitants decided to protect themselves. They formed an association with a committee of management. One of the rules was that every member should provide himself with 'a good musket, a bayonet, a brace of

Maori bargaining with a trader in the 1840s.

pistols, a cutlass and at least sixty rounds of ball cartridge'. Kororareka was a wild frontier town!

The Hokianga had a dangerous sand bar two and a half kilometres from the entrance to the harbour. Once over the bar, however, ships could find shelter and navigate right up to Horeke, where there was a shipyard and sawmill. Up to fifty men worked in the shipyard. Between 1827 and 1830 they built three large ships — the *Enterprise*, 40 tons, the *New Zealander*, 140 tons, and the *Sir George Murray*, 392 tons. Other sawmills were established on the many rivers that fed into the harbour. The work of logging the kauri was laborious and difficult, but the timber was in great demand. There was a thriving settlement on the Hokianga, with missions established by Methodists and Roman Catholics. Pakeha-Maori like Frederick Maning lived and traded with Maori communities. The Hokianga was the second-largest Pakeha settlement in New Zealand.

The experiences of James Caddell show that relationships between Maori and the traders were not always peaceful. James was thirteen years old in 1806 when he was landed with a group of sealers near South Cape. The ship *Sydney Cove* intended to come back for them when they had collected enough sealskins. Unfortunately, the party was attacked by Maori and all except James were killed and eaten. James had been about to be killed when he got away from the men holding him and ran up to a chief called Tako, and caught hold of his clothing. Tako was tapu at that time and that meant that no one could touch James without risking dreadful punishment. He was allowed to live. He grew up with the tribe and married the daughter of the chief. He became a chief himself and had his face tattooed. He fought in many wars with his tribe. When he met up with Europeans again he had almost forgotten his own language. Later he visited Sydney with his wife but decided he preferred living with his tribe in New Zealand and returned there.

Although incidents of violence occurred between Maori and traders, these were rare. Both groups had too much to gain from each other to want to break off contact. Traders did not wish to change Maori society, but their new goods and techniques did eventually bring about big changes.

The missionaries

The missionaries, however, did want to change Maori society. They did not normally live with the Maori as the Pakeha-Maori did. Their aim was to bring civilisation and Christianity to a heathen world. The Church Missionary Society, an Anglican organisation, under the direction of Samuel Marsden sent out a schoolmaster, a carpenter and a ropemaker in 1814 to establish a mission in the Bay of Islands. They made no converts until 1825 and were only welcomed because of the trade they brought. Hongi Hika said that Christianity was no good as a religion for warriors. Later, when the mission moved to Kerikeri and then to Waimate, and with the arrival of men like Henry Williams, William Colenso and Octavius Hadfield, the Church Missionary Society began to have more effect.

The Wesleyan Missionary Society was smaller. It set up a mission at Whangaroa and later moved to the Hokianga. There at Mangungu, near the Horeke sawmills, they established a small mission. There was also a Roman Catholic mission, established under Bishop Pompallier, first at the Hokianga and then at Kororareka.

There were never many missionaries at any one time. Most areas were not affected by them. At first they found it very difficult to make converts. They also found that they were sometimes obliged to trade in muskets like the traders they despised. However, they discovered when they translated the Bible, the Prayer Book and hymns into Maori that they had more success. Maori were keen to read and to write their own language.

Sometimes the missionaries' ignorance of Maori customs was dangerous. Mrs Williams described one instance in a letter in 1823. Elizabeth Puckey, the daughter of one of the Anglican missionaries, played with Hongi Hika's daughter. In an argument they traded insults about their fathers. Hongi Hika's daughter told Elizabeth that her father was not a rangatira as her own was. She said that when her father came back from England he would cut off Mr Puckey's head and put it in the frying pan. Elizabeth replied that her father would cut off Hongi Hika's head and put it in the pot. This was a deadly insult to a proud Maori chief. When Hongi Hika returned from England he sent a raiding party to revenge the insult. The Puckey family were lucky to lose only their possessions instead of their lives.

A mission station usually had a house for the missionary's family, a chapel for worship, a schoolroom and sometimes sleeping quarters for the children and adults being taught or trained as teachers. Supplies came from the mission farm

Samuel Marsden, founder of the Church Missionary Society, arrived in the Bay of Islands in 1814. He set up an Anglican mission station.

The mission settlement at Waimate North. The mission house flew a flag, bearing a dove, a cross and the word 'rongopai' (good news). Bishop Selwyn lived here from 1843 to 1844.

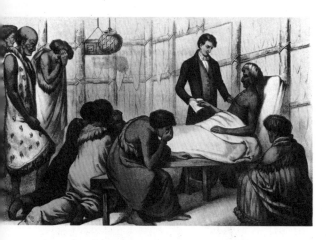

A missionary visits a dying Maori chief.

and orchard, supplemented by food bought from the Maori villages.

William Colenso set up a small printing press and could hardly keep up with the demand for Bibles. Knowledge of Christianity was often spread by slaves who had been captured by the Ngapuhi on their raids, then freed by the missionaries and returned to their tribes. It was not until the Maori gods seemed unable to protect their people from the terrible diseases and evils of the Pakeha that Maori were prepared to accept the Christian God. Often it would be one part of Christian teaching that would be accepted, such as treating Sunday as a day of rest. Traditional religious beliefs were altered to fit in with the new ideas. Some of the new ideas meant that Maori social life had to change. Missionaries discouraged polygamy (chiefs having more than one wife) and did their best to stop cannibalism.

Change in Maori society

Missionaries tried consciously to change Maori culture, but the new products and ideas brought by both traders and missionaries changed Maori society much more.

The better yield of the potato meant that less time had to be spent cultivating the food crop and more time could be spent fighting. Hand-to-hand fighting had meant that Maori war casualties were slight. The musket made tribal fighting much more devastating. A tribe armed with muskets could raid areas further from home because they were less likely to be ambushed. Warriors like Hongi Hika were able to lead expeditions from the Bay of Islands down to Rotorua, inflicting terrible defeats on the defending tribes.

Te Rauparaha, a chief then living in the Wellington area, crossed Cook Strait and raided the South Island tribes. These musket wars disrupted Maori society greatly. Many people were killed and the demand for muskets for protection and revenge increased. Thousands of Maori moved to different areas to live because of the fighting, and this made later land claims very complicated.

Once most Maori had muskets the fighting died down and by 1830 the tribes were generally at peace with each other.

A worse killer than the musket was European disease. For hundreds of years Maori had lived isolated from other races and had little immunity from common European sicknesses. Now, even the common cold or measles could be devastating.

The demand for flax also had bad effects on health. The flax collectors moved down to live near the damp, unhealthy swamps to make the task easier, but their health often suffered as a result.

Traditional Maori tools were made of stone and wood. The Europeans arrived with iron tools and metals unavailable in New Zealand. They introduced new technology. Books, clocks, compasses and money were completely new ideas. Not all these material goods were beneficial. Axes could be used to kill. Alcohol was often misused. Augustus Earle tells the sad tale of a Maori who did not know the properties of gunpowder:

> A few months since, a native came from the interior driving a quantity of pigs to barter for powder; he obtained several pounds weight, and set off to return home. On his journey he passed the night in a hut, and for safety put the bag of powder under his head for a pillow; and as a New Zealander always sleeps with a fire close to him, the consequence was, in the course of the night the fire communicated to the powder and destroyed the man and the whole of his family, who were journeying with him.

But Maori culture and economy had begun to be part of a wider economy and culture. Barter was giving way to exchanges of goods for cash.

All these new developments were very uneven in their effect. The tribes of the north, like the Ngapuhi, were the most directly affected. The tribes of the central North Island were much less affected.

Many of the Pakeha who came to New Zealand in this period did not mean to stay, but the changes they brought with them were already having a permanent effect upon Maori life.

Archdeacon Williams and his brother being approached by a group of Maori threatening to destroy their potato crop. Sometimes the missionaries offended the Maori without realising they had done so.

FIVE

Under the British Flag

I n 1830 there had been no more than 300 to 330 Europeans living in New Zealand. By 1840 this number increased to 2,000. Most of them had come to stay.

Imports and exports had more than doubled. Reports of the mild climate, the good farming land, and the co-operation of the Maori had begun to attract new settlers in increasing numbers. Most came from New South Wales, which had been suffering from the effects of drought, low prices for wool and high prices for land. New Zealand sounded much more attractive to a new settler.

The British Government in New South Wales had been very concerned about affairs in New Zealand for some time. People who committed crimes in New Zealand could be tried in New South Wales, but this had not stopped some very bad crimes. One shocking case was that of Captain Stewart of the brig *Elizabeth.* In 1830, in return for a cargo of flax, he carried on board his ship Te Rauparaha and a war party from Kapiti Island to Akaroa. There, Captain Stewart helped Te Rauparaha lure his tribal enemy, Tamaiharanui of the Ngai Tahu tribe, onto the ship. Tamaiharanui brought his eleven-year-old daughter, Nga Roimata, with him. Te Rauparaha made them prisoners and burned and sacked their village, killing all the people he could find. They sailed back to Kapiti with fifty prisoners, including Tamaiharanui and his daughter. Tamaiharanui knew that he and his daughter could expect no mercy from Te Rauparaha, and so he strangled his daughter himself and threw her body into the sea. He was right in his prediction, for the rest of the prisoners, including Tamaiharanui himself, were tortured to death. Captain Stewart was later charged in a Sydney court with helping Te Rauparaha, but all the witnesses had disappeared and the case had to be abandoned.

Te Rauparaha drawn by Edward Abbott in 1845. He was a famous chief of the Ngati Toa.

James Busby — British Resident

Concern over cases like this led to the appointment of a British Resident for New Zealand in 1833. This was James Busby, called by Maori the 'man-o-war without guns'. Busby encouraged Maori chiefs at Waitangi to choose a flag, the first New Zealand national flag. It measured five metres by three metres, and had a red St George's Cross on a white ground and four eight-point stars. The flag was hoisted and the HMS *Alligator*, anchored offshore, gave it a twenty-one-gun salute. However, Busby found it very difficult to enforce his authority. He had no soldiers or legal powers. The British Government in New South Wales did not want the extra expense of sending troops to New Zealand.

Bishop Pompallier, the leader of the Catholic Church in New Zealand. He arrived in this country in 1838.

When Busby's own house was raided and his store of food and supplies was ransacked by the Maori he could do nothing. Even the missionaries seemed to have more standing or, as the Maori expressed it, mana.

From time to time the British navy visited the coast of New Zealand to settle disputes and to show that it did not pay to harm British subjects. The French navy also visited New Zealand to demonstrate their support for the French leader of the Roman Catholic mission, Bishop Pompallier. This worried those who felt that New Zealand should be British. In 1837 their anti-French fears were increased by the claims of a rather strange Frenchman — Baron Charles de Thierry, who announced that he intended to be Sovereign Chief of New Zealand. His large blue and crimson silken flag rivalled the flag chosen by the Maori chiefs. He claimed to have purchased 40,000 acres of land in the Hokianga. Although his claims were wild, he did have connections with the French Court. The French never appeared to take him seriously, but Busby was sufficiently worried to call together thirty-four of the northern chiefs at Waitangi. This gathering proclaimed the country to be independent and asked the British government for protection. Busby was probably doing what he could to build up his own position.

The reports of the missionaries and settlers seemed to show that law and order was a major problem in New Zealand at this time. James Busby sent his superiors a report claiming that there was no order or stability in New Zealand. Such claims are difficult to check. Although the musket wars had disrupted Maori society, the worst of the warfare was well over. Certainly, European diseases had caused the Maori population to decline, but no one was sure by how much. However, it was also clear that the economy was prospering and that many more settlers were arriving, which they certainly would not have done if things were as bad as Busby suggested.

Edward Gibbon Wakefield

One of those who hoped to make his fortune by settling immigrants in the new land was Edward Gibbon Wakefield. His early life had been full of excitement. First he tried making his fortune by marrying an heiress. After the death of his first wife he carried off Ellen Turner, a schoolgirl and the daughter of a wealthy manufacturer. Wakefield married her at Gretna Green in Scotland, where marriage laws were not as strict as in England. Ellen's family chased them to France, and had Wakefield and his brother William arrested. They were sentenced by the court to three years' imprisonment in Newgate gaol.

Edward Gibbon Wakefield, founder of the New Zealand Company.

Ellen Turner, the young heiress abducted from school by Edward Gibbon Wakefield in 1826.

While Edward Wakefield was in prison he worked out his ideas about colonising and settling new countries. He hoped to found a new colony in New Zealand. He thought new settlement should be carefully planned and not just allowed to develop in a haphazard way. If closely settled farming communities were set up, new settlers would not spread out over the whole country and it would be much easier to provide them with schools, churches and halls. Behind Wakefield's ideas was the hope that his company could buy Maori land very cheaply. This land would then be sold at a high price to wealthy men. The profits would be used to pay the fares of carefully chosen labourers who wanted to emigrate to the new country. These labourers would have to work for some years before they saved enough to buy land for themselves. As a result there would be plenty of labour available for the new farmers.

Wakefield's scheme would mean that the new colony would be a copy of an English farming area. Landowners would be people of status and privilege. Like English gentlemen, they would not need to work with their hands. Labourers would do the work on the farms. Wakefield felt it was important to have land highly enough priced so that it was out of reach of most of the workers.

The New Zealand Company

In 1838 Wakefield formed a company to put his ideas into practice. The New Zealand Company offered land in New Zealand for sale in London. None of the buyers, either speculators or genuine farmers, had seen the land they were buying. In fact, the Company itself had not completed buying the land. The land had not been surveyed or examined to see if it was suitable for farming. The Company hoped to make big profits by selling land in the Wellington area. This was the area they expected to become the capital of New Zealand.

Wakefield was in a great hurry to get his new settlers off to New Zealand. Rumours were spreading that the British Government was about to annex New Zealand. If that happened, it was likely that the new government would take control of all the land. Wakefield's chance to buy land very cheaply would be at risk. The Company quickly sent the ship *Tory* to New Zealand, with surveyors and land buyers aboard. Captain Arthur Wakefield, another of Edward Wakefield's brothers, was in charge.

All this activity stirred the British Government into action and William Hobson, a naval captain, was sent to New Zealand. His instructions were to persuade the Maori chiefs to recognise Queen Victoria's authority so that New Zealand would be governed by Britain. He was also given permission, if it proved necessary, to claim the South Island. This claim would be based on the British discovery of New Zealand. Captain Hobson arrived in the Bay of Islands on 29 January 1840. He was to be the Lieutenant-Governor of New Zealand under the authority of the Governor of New South Wales.

Speculators

These were people who did not intend to farm the land themselves. They bought land in order to sell it later when it would have increased in value. Their aim was to make money from buying land when it was cheap and selling it when it was expensive.

Annex

When one government takes over control of another country or part of a country.

The Treaty of Waitangi

Hobson summoned Maori chiefs to a meeting at Waitangi on 5 February 1840. According to his instructions, he and his staff drew up a document, called the Treaty of Waitangi, to put to the chiefs. Hobson wanted the Maori chiefs to agree to Great Britain's taking the responsibility for governing the northern part of New Zealand. The chiefs were asked to give up to the Queen the right to buy their land. In return, their possession of land and property was to be guaranteed and they were to have all the rights and privileges of British subjects.

Early on the morning of 5 February Maori began gathering on the lawn at Waitangi. It was a particularly beautiful day. Canoes could be seen gliding towards Waitangi from every direction. In the middle of each canoe stood the kaituki (canoe song singer). With gestures and chants each kaituki stirred the rowers along so that they kept time with his rhythm. Boats with settlers and residents landed on the shore. Ships at anchor in the bay were decorated with the flags of their nations.

On the lawn there was a large tent draped with flags, with the English flag fluttering proudly in the breeze. Everything looked cheerful and pleasant. Even the cicadas sang more loudly than ever.

The French Roman Catholic bishop, Bishop Pompallier, arrived dressed in his formal clerical clothes. He looked very grand with his massive gold chain and crucifix glistening on his dark-purple coloured gown. The Maori were most impressed: 'Ko ia ano te tino rangatira!' ('He indeed, is the chief gentleman!') This upset the Protestant missionaries, who were dressed in dull black. They were worried that they might be upstaged by the Bishop. They felt that the Maori might think Catholics were more important than Protestants.

The Maori chiefs looked splendid. Some were dressed in dogskin mats of black-and-white stripes. Others were wearing new woollen cloaks of crimson, blue, brown, and plaid. Some were dressed in plain European clothes, others were wearing traditional Maori dress.

The chief of the Rarawa tribe, Hakitara, was wearing a very large and handsome silky white kaitaka mat, worn only by superior chiefs. It was fringed with a dark-coloured woven border with a zig-zag pattern. The sunlight on the beautiful white cloak made him stand out from the other chiefs. Here and there, taiaha, symbols of rank, had been thrust into the ground. They were adorned with the long flowing white hair from the tail of the New Zealand dog, and with crimson cloth and red feathers. Many of the Maori wore snow-white feathers in their glossy black hair. The Pakeha, who were dressed very soberly, looked quite different.

A day of speeches followed. Hobson explained the terms of the treaty and why it was necessary. Many powerful chiefs opposed the treaty. A few wanted to return to the days before the Pakeha brought blankets, bread, muskets and disease. Some said that if this new government stayed, their dignity would be lost. They would be as low as worms, they would be like slaves.

One of these chiefs was Tareha, a chief of the Ngati Rehia (Ngapuhi) tribe. He was a very tall and robust man, the biggest Maori in the whole district, and made his point very dramatically. Tareha demonstrated his attitude by deliberately dressing in a filthy piece of coarse old floor matting, loosely tied around him. He carried in his hand, by a string, a bunch of dried fern root. He ridiculed those Maori who were tempted by foreign goods. In his deep, powerful voice, he cried out to the Pakeha:

> Go back, return; make haste away. See, this is my food, the food of my ancestors.
> . . . To think of tempting men — us Natives — with baits of clothing and of food!

Tamati Waka Nene, a Ngapuhi chief, replied to those who opposed the Treaty of Waitangi. He said that it was too late to turn the white men away. Those who did not want to sign the treaty should have sent the traders home a generation before. He called on Hobson to stay, to preserve Maori customs, to protect the ownership of their lands and to save them from slavery. Very dramatically he cried out: 'Stay thou, our friend, our father, our Governor!'

Signing the treaty

The following day the chiefs were asked to sign the treaty. At first no one would come forward. Then Busby hit on the idea of calling them out individually, starting with Hone Heke, who was known to be in favour of signing. Most signed the treaty, even those who had the day before opposed it. But before they signed, Colenso, the missionary printer, interrupted proceedings to say that he felt that the chiefs did not fully understand what they were going to sign. Hobson brushed him aside irritably and the signing proceeded.

The version of the treaty signed by the Maori chiefs was written in the Maori language. It had been translated by Henry Williams who, like the other Pakeha giving advice to Hobson, was very concerned about protecting all the land he had bought. Williams claimed ownership of 11,000 acres. His translation used words that were not traditional Maori words but had been invented to describe ideas not part of the Maori culture. An example was the word 'kawanatanga' (governorship), which Williams used to describe the idea of rule or sovereignty. The more usual Maori word would be 'mana' and would have described more clearly what the chiefs were signing away. Henry Williams was the main translator and explained the treaty to the Maori at Waitangi. He used all his powers of persuasion to get them to sign, although one European there was heard to say that Williams was not translating a great deal to do with land and the missionaries.

It has been said that the Maori chiefs were not familiar with the legal language and traditions the document required. They were more interested in making sure no rival tribe used the opportunity to steal a march on them than looking carefully at the meaning of some of the clauses. In 1840, the year the treaty was signed, Maori outnumbered Pakeha in New Zealand by ten to one. They certainly could not imagine that within a generation the Maori population would fall rapidly and that the number of Pakeha would increase greatly.

A view of the Treaty House, Waitangi.

A reconstruction of the signing of the Treaty of Waitangi.

Disagreements over the treaty

Doubts over the true meaning of the Treaty of Waitangi do not stop there. The treaty was difficult to understand. Hobson drew it up in a hurry. He was not trained in law and he had no legal advisers with him. There is even some doubt over which of the texts is the important one. The Maori at Waitangi signed the Maori version, some Waikato chiefs later signed the English version. The two versions are not exactly the same. In the second clause, which promised the tribes, in the English version, 'full exclusive and undisturbed possession of their lands and estates, forests and fisheries . . .', the Maori version described it more vaguely as 'the entire chieftainship of their lands, their villages, and all their property'. The other area of later confusion was whether or not Maori had given the Crown the sole right to buy their land.

Nevertheless the treaty continues to have great importance for all New Zealanders. Although it was hastily drawn up, confusing and not very clear, there is one aspect of it that was important. This was put into words by Hobson himself, in the few Maori words he had learnt: 'He iwi tahi tatou.' (We are one people.)

It took several months to collect signatures from Maori chiefs. Meanwhile the New Zealand Company settlers at Port Nicholson (Wellington) had formed a government, appointed magistrates and were making their own laws. To put a stop to this, Hobson issued a proclamation on 21 May 1840, which got the approval of the Queen and established British sovereignty over the whole of New Zealand.

This proclamation established British sovereignty over the whole of New Zealand.

SIX

The Early Governors and the Maori

Governor Robert FitzRoy.

The Governors of New Zealand were (and still are) the representatives of the Queen. In the early days they had to carry out the orders of the British Government. But in practice they were in charge. When a Governor wrote a report to the Colonial Office in London, it might take several months to arrive by sailing ship. By the time a reply was received, perhaps giving instructions, further months would go by. So decisions often had to be made by the man on the spot — the Governor.

Governor FitzRoy

The first Governor, William Hobson, died in 1842. His grave is by Grafton Bridge in Auckland. He was followed by another naval officer, Robert FitzRoy. He did not prove to be a successful governor. But we need to remember that some of his main troubles were military, and he had begun with only about a hundred soldiers — hardly enough to beat a single Maori hapu.

Governor FitzRoy arrived to find trouble waiting for him. It was one thing to hope for peace between Maori and settlers, as Governor Hobson had at Waitangi. It was another to achieve it. Seeing settlers arriving in large numbers at Wellington and elsewhere, many Maori began to fear for their future. The settlers knew nothing of Maori customs and cared less. The New Zealand Company had been very careless in buying Maori land, and many Maori owners now denied that they had sold. There was trouble as settlers moved onto land near Wellington and also in Nelson.

Trouble at Wairau

An example of the conflicts between Maori and settlers at this time was the Wairau dispute. The great chiefs Te Rauparaha and Te Rangihaeata said that they had not sold the land there, which they had conquered in the 1820s. But in 1843 the settlers ignored the chiefs and began to survey the land. When the two chiefs and their followers visited the area, they said that they would not permit the survey until the ownership had been looked into by William Spain, a lawyer who was investigating early land sales for the government. It is now clear that many of the owners had not sold.

When the surveyors went ahead the Maori burned their huts. The Company now sent an armed party of thirty-five men to arrest Te Rauparaha. He and his party had occupied a good position up a hill, with bush behind. To threaten those two chiefs, experienced and ruthless in warfare, with a handful of men with no military training was an act of incredible stupidity. Te Rauparaha naturally declined to give himself up. One of the settlers shot and killed Te Rongo, wife of Te Rangihaeata. The Maori then shot or tomahawked twenty-two of the Europeans, including Captain Arthur Wakefield.

Hone Heke (centre) with his wife, Harriett, and Kawiti.

When FitzRoy arrived he did not have enough troops to tackle Te Rauparaha. In any case he believed that the settlers had been in the wrong, and he decided to do nothing. But soon FitzRoy was faced with a more difficult problem. There was trouble at the Bay of Islands, not because of settlers arriving, but partly because they were leaving — to go to the new capital, Auckland. Land sales dropped as the settlers left. The Governor had introduced customs duties (taxes on imports) which discouraged trade. In the north many Maori found that they were poorer, and they blamed the new government. Some of them, like Hone Heke, a nephew of the great Hongi Hika, began to fear that the Pakeha, the white settlers, would take all their land.

Hone Heke

Heke had been the first person to sign the Treaty of Waitangi, but now he said that he had been tricked. Americans living at the Bay of Islands told the Maori how bad the British were and how cruelly they had treated the native people in Australia. Heke started to fly an American flag on his war canoe. He decided to get rid of the British flag, the sign of British rule, which flew at Waitangi. Heke

Tamati Waka Nene, chief of the Ngapuhi.

and his people cut down the flagstaff. Some of them must have thought that this was great sport. Three times the Pakeha put the flagstaff up and three times the Maori cut it down. An armed guard was placed by the fourth flagstaff. This time the Maori attacked the troops and sacked and burned Kororareka after most of the inhabitants had fled. New Zealand's first European town was a smoking ruin. Fifteen soldiers and sailors and perhaps thirteen Maori were dead.

For the British, Heke's success was a terrible shock. 'Neither I nor anyone else,' wrote Governor Fitz-Roy, 'thought of his succeeding in an attack on our forces.'

Hone Heke was not a senior chief. Nevertheless, he had about 300 men, while his ally Kawiti had another 150. The great Ngapuhi chief Tamati Waka Nene and his friends, with 400 men, sided with the British. He said that the war was not about the land; if it had been he would not have fought against Heke.

More troops were sent from Sydney. There were about 400 soldiers, sailors and marines. The government forces now attacked one of Hone Heke's pa, near Lake Omapere. They charged towards the Maori stockades of puriri trunks with their bayonets. Kawiti and his men attacked them in the open. Fourteen British were killed and at least as many Maori. But it was another Maori victory — the troops had to retreat. The Ngapuhi were impressed by the soldiers' courage at this battle, and also by their bad language. The Maori were very surprised to hear the troops swearing and cursing at them. Worse was to follow. Fighting continued between the followers of Waka Nene and Hone Heke. In one engagement Heke was badly wounded in the thigh, but recovered, the Maori believed, with the help of a tohunga (priest), and Te Atua Wera (The Red God).

FitzRoy received reinforcements and the troops went to attack a strong pa that Heke and Kawiti had occupied and strengthened at Ohaeawai. It was surrounded by three lines of wooden walls and covered on the outside with green flax, which could stop bullets. Inside were many pits and trenches. Artillery fire had little effect on the pa and its defenders. The troops outnumbered the Maori about six to one and the commanding officer, Colonel H. Despard, decided to storm the pa with a bayonet charge. Waka Nene said he was a 'very stupid man', and although someone translated the Maori words into English for Despard, he took no notice.

The British charged in four ranks, a pace apart, straight into the Maori muskets. Despite their incredible courage, the soldiers were mown down by the concealed Maori. Few got inside the Maori defences. None of those survived. Over 100 British were killed or wounded, and perhaps ten Maori. One Maori warrior said,

'The soldiers fell on this side and that, like so many sticks thrown down.' It was another humiliating defeat for the British, as both sides knew.

Governor FitzRoy was withdrawn (that is, given the sack). He had been a failure. Most of the settlers hated him. They thought he should have punished Te Rauparaha, but he had too few troops. He had also proved infirm in purpose, changing his mind as the wind changes.

Governor Grey

FitzRoy was replaced by a remarkable man, New Zealand's most famous Governor, this time an army officer — Captain (later Sir) George Grey. He had had an adventurous life. As a young English army officer Grey had served in Ireland, where he felt a great sympathy for the poor people. Much later, as a New Zealand politician and premier (prime minister), he was to make many fiery speeches about the bad deeds of landlords and owners of huge farms. In 1837 and 1838 he was a leader of

Governor Sir George Grey (about 1854).

an exploring expedition, far to the north of Perth, in Western Australia. The party had set off with twenty-six ponies, 'small untrained brutes', as 'untrained as their masters'. Everything went wrong. Some of their animals died, and hostile Aborigines hit Grey with three spears. He shot one of them in the arm.

I felt severely wounded in the hip but . . . as I fell, I heard the savage yells of the natives' delight and triumph; these recalled me to myself, and, roused by momentary rage and indignation, I made a strong effort, rallied, and in a moment was on my legs; the spear was wrenched from my wound, and my haversack drawn closely over it, that neither my own party nor the natives might see it, and I advanced again steadily to the rock. The man became alarmed, and threatened me with his club, yelling most furiously; but as I neared the rock . . . he fled . . . he was scarcely uncovered in his flight, when my rifle ball pierced him through the back, between the shoulders, and he fell heavily on his face with a deep groan.

The effect was electrical. The tumult of the combat had ceased: not another yell was uttered.

Grey's courage saved his party. He wrote to his mother, 'I do not think that since the days of Robinson Crusoe, anyone has been through so much personal adventure as I have lately undergone.'

He led another unsuccessful exploring party and was then appointed Governor of South Australia, another colony begun by Edward Gibbon Wakefield. Grey's reputation was now high in London and in 1845 he was sent to govern war-torn

New Zealand. He was thirty-three years old. Most of the early New Zealand leaders were young by modern standards. Few old people could stand the long sea voyage — the longest route for migrants in the world — of several months.

Grey was given what had been refused Hobson and FitzRoy, a generous number of troops. Some army officers and other people had greatly underestimated the skill and courage of the Maori, holding that one English soldier was worth six Maori. A politician was later heard to say that he could cut his way from Auckland to Wellington with a regiment of Indian troops. The idea was ridiculous. They would not have passed the Waikato River alive.

By early 1846 Grey had over 1,000 men, while Waka Nene had a further 400 or 500. They moved in and fired an artillery barrage at Kawiti's pa, Ruapekape-ka (the Bat's Nest). Kawiti and Hone Heke (who had joined him there) escaped. There were some casualties on both sides.

Heke, who had been educated at the Anglican mission, wrote to Governor Grey that FitzRoy had had no right to the land: 'Because God made this country for us it cannot be sliced — if it were a whale it might be sliced — but as for this — do you return to your own country, to England which was made by God for you. God has made this country for us. . . .' The letter finished with a war song: 'Oh let us fight, fight, fight, aha! Let us fight for the land which lies before us.'

Grey decided to make peace with Heke. He wisely decided not to follow up the threats FitzRoy had made that the land of 'rebels' would be confiscated. This would have stirred the Maori to fight on.

There was further trouble near Wellington, in the Hutt Valley and elsewhere over settlers occupying land that Maori denied selling. The militia began building stockades, blockhouses, or forts, like those built in the USA for defence against the Indians. The walls were large slabs of timber. One of these, a barn surrounded by a stockade, was built in a bush clearing on Mr Boulcott's farm, up the Hutt River. In May 1846 it

Fort Richmond and the Hutt Bridge (1847).

was attacked, on the order of Te Rangihaeata, by a party of Maori. A sentry saw them and fired one shot before he was tomahawked. The bugler, a young fellow named William Allen, seized his bugle to sound the alarm. A Maori tomahawked him in the shoulder. He took the bugle in his left hand but was killed before he could blow it. All of the guards were shot, but the rest of the garrison were now awake. Soldiers and militia fought the Maori until they retreated.

Later in the morning a youth of seventeen, John Cuddy, was driving a cart loaded with food towards the camp when two men, driving a cart furiously away from it, shouted to him, 'Go back, boy, go back! The Maori have attacked.'

'I dursen't go back,' he cried. 'I've got the rations to deliver.'

When he reached the camp he found six dead men, including Bugler Allen.

The capture of Te Rauparaha

Grey sent most of the troops and several men-of-war down to Wellington. As in the north, some of the local tribes, including the Ngati Awa, helped the British.

Grey believed that Te Rauparaha was behind the attacks in the south, so he decided to capture him. He sailed in a steamer, the *Driver,* and headed south, past Te Rauparaha's pa (near modern Plimmerton) as though making for Wellington, and then turned back. At dawn troops and sailors landed and seized Te Rauparaha while he was asleep. Grey then kept him in prison, without laying any charges, or giving him a trial.

History is not all 'facts'. We could argue forever about whether Grey's action was right. What is certain is that the mana of Te Rauparaha, his prestige and power, declined and Grey's rose like the morning sun.

Te Rangihaeata was forced out of his pa by troops and the 'friendlies' (friendly Maori). He fled into the hills above Horokiwi. Soon the fight was, for the time being, over.

Eliza Grey writes home

While Grey experienced the excitements of war, his young wife Eliza grew bored and discontented in Government House at Auckland. She wrote to a friend, Maggie Watts:

> I am feeling very feverish and ill — and here I am quite alone, Maggie — my husband some hundred miles away — and perfect strangers round here — 'twould be rather unpleasant to be ill under such circumstances, would it not — and I was so ill when I landed — and continued so all last week, that I was unable to receive my new subjects so that I scarce know any one by sight even. I have been very busy today making out a list of all my wants to send to Sydney — for I am without the common necessaries of life — in the way of furniture — nothing can be bought here.

A few months later she wrote to her friend again:

> I really ought to be accustomed to live alone by this time. I am so constantly left now — and I am growing graver and gloomier than ever I fear. The country, place and (up to now) the people are very distasteful to me — there is scarcely a lady here — and were it not for the large military and naval force stationed here, there would scarcely be a Gentleman.

She added that she wished that she had 'only advanced a little more in years so as to be more independent, and less talkable about. I should be better off.' She said that the Maori regarded her 'with great contempt' and called her 'a mere child'. It was very difficult for anyone to get used to such a new life.

Grey and the Maori

Lady Grey, who wrote to a friend in England: 'I am growing graver and gloomier than ever I fear.'

During his first governorship of New Zealand, from 1845 to 1853, Grey got on very well with many important Maori. The chiefs visited him. He learned to speak Maori and persuaded some of the chiefs to write down the legends and other stories of the Maori. He translated these into English and published a book, first of all in Maori, *Ko Nga Mahinga a nga Tupuna Maori* (The Deeds of the Maori Ancestors), and then his own English translation, *Mythology and Traditions of the New Zealanders*.

Governor Grey did his best to carry out the promise of the Treaty of Waitangi — that the Maori should be equal to the British. For instance, he gave money to some of the mission schools where hundreds of Maori learned to read, write and add. He built four hospitals for the Maori. He kept a firm control over purchases of Maori land to make sure that they were fair. The government agents who went round buying Maori land would discuss at a tribal meeting the boundaries and price of land to be bought. Sometimes several hundred Maori would sign the deed of sale, showing that they agreed.

Grey lent money to Maori tribes so that they could purchase ploughs and other farming equipment and flour mills. He said that they always repaid the money. Some Maori tribes became rich. In the Waikato there were many flour mills, making flour for the settlers. The Maori bought many coastal ships. In their canoes and ships they brought their wheat, flour and other produce to Auckland and Onehunga.

Governor Grey wrote to the Colonial Office in London that Maori and settlers had the same religion. They played the same sports. Indeed, he said, they already formed 'one people'. That was what Hobson had said at Waitangi. It was not true.

Grey's mana was probably higher among the Maori than among the settlers. The latter did not trust him. They thought that they could govern New Zealand better than he could. In 1846 the British Government sent out a constitution for New Zealand, that is, a document setting out a system of government. There were to be two Provincial Assemblies (parliaments) and a General Assembly (as there is now) for the whole country.

The Governor considered that the country was too unsettled to give the power to govern to the settlers. There was still fighting in Wanganui. To the fury of the settlers, he induced the British Government to put off introducing the constitution. The settlers called him the 'great dictator'. Yet he was to become the main author of the 1852 constitution, which set up what seemed in those days a democratic system of government. Most white men could vote, but no women. There were elected assemblies in each province and a General Assembly, which first met in Auckland in 1854. By this time Grey had gone off to be Governor of Cape Province in South Africa.

SEVEN

A New Life in a New Land

T he first emigrants boarded their ships with high hopes. A new life lay ahead. Their families would have better opportunities. There might be the chance to buy their own land. Even the thought of leaving relatives behind, perhaps for ever, to go to the other side of the world, did not deter them.

Those with a paid passage to New Zealand were carefully chosen. They had to be skilled workers, healthy and prepared to work hard. One of these was David Home, who had his passage paid by the New Zealand Manakau and Waitemata Company in 1840. In return he agreed to work for the company as a farm overseer or ploughman for twelve months at a wage between twenty-five and fifty cents a day, with board and lodging provided. He had to provide references as to his good character. The minister of his parish described how David had managed the small family farm after his father died. He had

New opportunities for a better life attracted many new settlers. This cartoon appeared in the English magazine Punch *in 1848.*

HERE   AND   THERE.

looked after his mother, brothers and sisters. The high rent and poor soil had made it difficult, so David had to leave the parish to earn more money. The minister recommended David to the company as a 'steady, sober, well-behaved young man', and as a 'fit and trustworthy person to be employed as overseer on a farm'. The minister described David as one who could learn other jobs if he had to. This was a quality which all new settlers needed.

Shipboard life for the emigrants

The New Zealand Company emigrants, also carefully selected, were told what they would need on board ship. They were issued with a mattress, pillow and cooking pots. They had to provide their own blankets, sheets and covers; their own knives, forks, plates, spoons and a large pewter or tin drinking mug. Each family had to have a linen bag large enough to hold a month's supply of clothing. The rest of their luggage was stowed in the hold. Company officials checked that they had enough plain, strong clothing and the tools of their trade. The emigrants could buy the clothes and equipment they would need from the New Zealand Company's office in London.

SHIPS FOR NEW ZEALAND,
for the Conveyance of Passengers and Stores to the Settlement of Otago.

New Zealand House,
22nd September, 1847.

The Court of Directors of the *New Zealand Company* do hereby give notice that they will be ready on Thursday, the 30th day of September instant, at One o'clock precisely, to receive Tenders at *New Zealand House*, for the hire of two Ships, of not less than 450, nor above 650 Tons each, old measurement, to be ready to sail on the 30th day of October, 1847, the one from Port or Ports in the Clyde, and the other from the Port of London, to Otago, in New Zealand.

The Tenders to be made according to a Form, which may be had on application at New Zealand House, 9, Broad Street Buildings, London, and at 3, West Nile Street, Glasgow.

The Directors do not pledge themselves to accept the lowest, or any tender.

The New Zealand Company hired ships to carry the new settlers to New Zealand.

Steerage passengers were organised into cooking groups or messes. Each one was issued with food according to a set scale. The ration for one adult was:

3/4 lb biscuit a day,
1 lb Indian beef (Tuesday and Saturday only),
1/2 lb pork three times a week,
1/2 lb preserved meat twice a week,
1/2 lb flour and 1/2 pint peas a day,
1/4 lb rice and 3/4 lb potatoes four times a week,
plus butter, sugar, tea, coffee, raisins, suet, pickled cabbage, salt, mustard and water.

Children received part of an adult's ration. Those under twelve months were not entitled to rations. If a mess did not use all its rations during the voyage, they would receive what was left when they arrived in the colony.

Proper medicines and medical comforts were carried on board the ship. These included twelve bottles of port wine, twelve bottles of sherry, 300 gallons of stout and forty gallons of brandy per hundred passengers. Oatmeal, arrowroot and lemon juice were also available. Women who were breast-feeding were issued with a pint of stout a day.

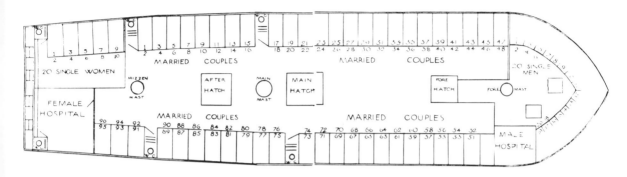

PLAN — LOWER DECK — SHIP BOLTON — 540 TONS
SAILED FROM GRAVESEND — OCTOBER — 1841

Steerage passengers were crowded into small enclosures in the ships' holds.

The voyage to New Zealand took four months, or longer if the ship struck bad weather. It was crowded and uncomfortable on board and the new settlers had to be patient and well-organised. The ships leaked, fresh food was scarce and illness was a constant worry. With no fresh water for washing, only the young men were bold enough to be hosed down on deck with sea-water. If a squall hit the ship, the young male passengers were called out to help shorten sail. When the sailors hoisted the sails they would all pull together to shanties like this:

Life on board emigrant ships was crowded, uncomfortable and lacking in privacy.

> *Oh, once I had a little dog*
> *His name was Judy Callaghan*
> *Haul away! Haul away Joe!*

SCALE OF EMIGRANTS' OUTFIT

The Articles may be obtained by payment of the under-mentioned Prices, at the Company's Office (Emigration Department), or of Messrs. Dixon and Co., No. 12 Fenchurch Street, London.

N.B. No other mattrasses, or bedding, will be allowed to be shipped, except such as have been approved by the Company as understated.

For each Adult Male

	s.	d.
2 Fustian Jackets, lined, at	5	6 each
2 Pair do. Trowsers, at 4s.3d. Lined, at	5	3 each
2 Do. Duck do., at	2	3 each
2 Round Frocks, at	2	5 each
12 Cotton Shirts, at	2	0 each
6 Pair Worsted Stockings, at	1	6 per pair
2 Scottish Caps, at	0	11 each
6 Handkerchiefs, at	0	8 each
6 Coarse Towels, at	0	7 each
1 pair Boots, with Hobnails, &c., at	7	6 per pair
1 Pair Shoes, at	5	3 per pair
4 lbs. Soap, at	0	8 per lb.
1 Pair Blankets, at	12	0 per pair
2 Pair Sheets, at	5	6 per pair
1 Coverlet, at	3	0 each

For each Adult Female

	s.	d.
2 Gowns, or 18 yards Printed Cotton, at	0	5½ per yard
2 Petticoats, or 6 yards Coloured Calico, at	0	5½ per yard
2 Do. Flannel, or 6 yards Flannel, at	1	2 per yard
12 Shifts, or 30 yards Long Cloth, at	0	6 per yard
6 caps, or 3 yards Muslin, at	1	0 per yard
6 Handkerchiefs, at	0	8 each
6 Aprons, or 6 yards Check, at	0	8 per yard
6 Neckerchiefs, at	0	8 each
6 Towels, at	0	7 each
1 pair Stays, at	3	6 each
6 Pair black Worsted Stockings, at	1	2 each
2 Pair Shoes, at	3	6 each
1 Bonnet, at	2	0 each
Needles, Pins, Buttons, Thread, Tape, &c., an assortment of	2	0
4 lbs. Marine Soap, at	0	8 per lb.
2 lbs. Starch, at	0	8 per lb.

	s.	d.
One Mattrass and Bolster for each couple, of coloured Wool	11	0
Knife and Fork, Plate, Spoon, Drinking Mug &c., say	3	0

Children must be provided with a proportionate Outfit, including Mattrass, &c., which may be had upon payment of the undermentioned Sum for each Child, viz:-

	£	s.	d.
One year of Age, and under Nine	1	0	0
Nine years of Age, and under Fourteen	1	10	0

On board ship there was a clear difference between those passengers who paid extra to have a cabin and those, usually assisted immigrants, who travelled steerage. The cabins were on the after deck, often raised above the main deck. Here the captain, the officers and a small number of passengers lived. A few sheep, crates of fowls, pigs and a cow were kept to supply the first-class passengers with fresh milk and meat.

The steerage passengers were in the hold, immediately below the main deck. There were no port-holes and the only light came from the open hatches, which were battened down in stormy weather. It was too dark to read or work below deck, and the air was very stuffy. Small enclosures of rough boards were provided for sleeping. A family of father, mother and four small children would sleep in an enclosure measuring 1.8 by 2.4 metres. In these conditions disease would often spread rapidly. It was the task of the ship's surgeon to control disease. In some ships his pay was cut every time someone died. It was often the small children who suffered most. The worst example was the ship *Lloyds,* which sailed for Nelson in 1842. Sixty-five children died during the voyage. Eight died from whooping cough, the rest died from a combination of malnutrition, diarrhoea, exposure to wet and cold, and neglect. Even on better disciplined and properly run ships, the sad scene of small bodies being buried at sea was a common sight.

Life on board was highly organised. Everyone was up at 6.30 a.m. Floors and decks were sprinkled with chloride of lime to control disease. Morning worship was followed by school for the children. Meals were the highlight of the day, although on some ships passengers organised entertainments and activities as well. The day would end with evening worship. Usually those on board were heading for the same settlement and were able to make plans for their new life. They would draw up the rules for their new community.

Settling in

After such a long voyage the first sight of the mountains of New Zealand was a great relief. However, landing was often very disappointing. In 1840 the first thousand Wellington settlers landed on the Petone beach. Thick bush and swamps were all they could see. Their goods were heaped in piles on the sand. There was no shelter, and Colonel Wakefield had not bought any land for them to farm. Even a year later, after the arrival of still more immigrants, Wellington was described as a very gloomy sight, with just a few huts to welcome the new arrivals.

Within six years, 9,000 new settlers had arrived in New Zealand. They were scattered between four little settlements. Later, in Dunedin and Christchurch the new settlers stayed in special barracks until they were ready to build their own houses. Elsewhere, even tents were a luxury. A good tarpaulin stretched over poles was common. The first camps were in the open, with heaped clay sheltering the fire. Cooking was done in ships' dixies and camp ovens. William Martin wrote to his cousin in 1849 from Dunedin describing how to make 'damper' bread in these conditions:

> First make the dough, let it stand for two hours at the fire to rise, then take a spade and scrape out the bottom of the fire, then lay in the damper and cover it with ashes and again the red embers, let it lie for about two hours, take it out and beat it well with a towel to clean it of ashes, when we have an excellent loaf.

The first houses were raupo huts or little cottages measuring 3.6 by 4.2 metres, built of upright and cross poles and plastered clay.

Maori were most willing to trade food for European clothes and goods. They supplied the Wellington settlers with pigs, fish, potatoes and vegetables. In the Bay of Islands Bishop Selwyn's wife found that she could buy 'a large kete [a basket something

The landing of the first Otago immigrants in 1848. Captain Cargill leads the way.

Auckland in 1840. The first houses were sometimes huts or little cottages.

The first four ships arrive with the Canterbury settlers on 27 December, 1850. The ships were the Charlotte Jane, *the* Randolph, *the* Cressy, *and the* Sir George Seymour.

like a carpenter's tool basket], of anything; potatoes, kumara, peaches, Cape gooseberries, quinces, all alike were one shilling each'. The Europeans found that New Zealand was a rich land, with fish, wild pigs and birds available for those who could develop the new skills of hunting them. Many new settlers were from towns or cities and at first found this difficult.

It was also difficult to move from one settlement to the other. Without roads, each settlement was isolated. As more new settlers arrived they were helped by the 'old hands', who showed them how to make tea from the leaves of the manuka (the 'tea-tree'), how to shoot the fat wood-pigeon for food and how to cure fish by smoking it. They learnt to beware of the poisonous tutu berries. A Nelson settler fell sick and died after eating the berries, but the jury knew so little of the plant that their verdict on his death was 'Died by the visitation of God'. Tutu was also a danger to the imported animals.

Raupo huts were soon replaced by timber or stone houses with separate sleeping and living areas. The new settlers learnt to build their homes facing north to get the sun. By the 1860s grand houses or homesteads were being built, especially in the South Island, where farming was prospering. In towns, working-men's cottages were built. Unlike those in England, each could have some land around it.

Daily life

Clothes and shoes had to be imported and were in short supply. Children played barefoot, which would have horrified their English relatives. Working men wore brightly coloured check shirts, made of flannel, cotton or worsted. Wealthier men brought fine linen shirts, sometimes in large numbers, as part of their essential luggage. Seventy-two dress shirts and forty waistcoats would form part of a gentleman's wardrobe. Women wore skirts which hid their ankles, with lots of petticoats. Even though washing clothes was difficult, collars were starched and great pride was taken in being neatly dressed. On Sunday everyone wore their best clothes. All the settlements would hold church services, even though they

Raupo huts were soon replaced by timber houses. Here a woman watches her husband fix the chimney.

might have to be held in the woolshed or the courthouse. Children were expected to go to Sunday school, and many homes had regular Bible readings and said grace at meal times.

Many children did not go to school regularly. Each province was supposed to organise education. Nelson set up schools by levying every householder for most of the cost. Many parents could not afford the fees they had to pay. Some needed the children to work on the farm. Others needed the small amounts that the children earned, to help feed the family. Quite young children went out to work for wages. Alfred Stallard, aged nine, was sent out to work on a farm. Harriet Bracken, aged twelve, was paid two shillings (twenty cents) a week for housework for Mrs Norrie. Out of this wage she paid for her own schooling and shoes.

Children were very likely to die young. Diphtheria, whooping cough, typhoid fever and diarrhoea were very common diseases. Families were often large, but many children died in their first year of life.

The role of women

Women were very important in the new settlements. Men found that wresting a farm from the bush was almost impossible without a wife to help. Preparing the food, cooking, washing and home-making was a full-time occupation. There were many more men than women in New Zealand. Settlers warned young men coming to the colony that it was better to take an extra week to look for a wife than to find a special plough or a well-bred horse.

Most women in New Zealand married. Nearly all worked at home-making or helped on the family farm. Small girls were often trained as domestic servants, which was seen as a good preparation for marriage. Within the home women had a wider range of responsibilities than they would have had in England. They earned much-needed cash from the sale of their butter and dairy goods. Sometimes they had to take over the management of the farm if their husbands died or left them. Not only did they bring up the children, they were often responsible for educating them, because schools were often distant and fees expensive. With few hospitals and limited medical services it was usually the women who took charge of the sick. Sometimes even young girls had to take a lot of responsibility for looking after children and babycare. Sarah Higgins grew up in Nelson as the oldest woman in her family and therefore the one to take responsibility for helping other women with babycare. She later became a skilled midwife.

The early houses were made of local materials, like this South Island cottage.

Perhaps the most important role women played in the new society was that of moderating the hard-drinking, rough-spoken pioneer society. Women used their influence to stop men drinking too heavily, and they did their best to remind the men of the polite customs and social manners of the land that they had come from. They taught their daughters to play the piano, and their sons to take off their hats when speaking to a lady. They softened the impact of the tough life pioneers had to live. Sarah Selwyn commented later in her life:

Sarah Elizabeth Barker sewing, with her workbox beside her.

> I felt it to be desirable to keep so far as might be an atmosphere of polish among the young men . . . people so easily sank in those days into rude habits and rough demeanour in out-of-the-way places in the colonies, that I felt it a duty to help George's young staff in homey ways lest their influence should be lowered. So we assembled in evening attire at our tea without milk and our bread without butter and made ourselves agreeable according to our lights and behaved 'pretty' as the nurses used to say — all you see with a real end.

Charlotte Godley took the matter even further. When two young men she knew were about to take up a sheep station in Canterbury in 1852, she warned them that they would become 'semi-barbarous'. She begged them to have 'a lay figure of a lady, carefully draped, set up in their usual sitting room, and always behave before it as if it were their mother'.

EIGHT

Earning a Living

In 1848 the Free Church of Scotland adapted Wakefield's ideas and settled immigrants in Otago. The Church of England did the same in Canterbury in 1850. In these settlements, as in those of the New Zealand Company, there were more workmen than there were jobs. The men and their families had to be settled on bush sections or vacant land. At first it was a struggle to grow enough food for their families. They found that arable farming (that is, growing crops for sale) was not a very profitable way of earning a living. Those with more money were able to import stock and graze cattle.

Sheep farming

A few enterprising settlers brought sheep over from Australia. One of the first of the large flocks was landed in Wellington in 1844 by Charles Clifford, and driven around the rocks of Baring Head and Palliser Bay up to the plains of the Wairarapa. At Mukamukaiti the drovers had to stand in the sea and pass the sheep from hand to hand around the rocks. The sheep had to be ferried across Lake Wairarapa to get to the cheaply leased grazing land beyond.

In spite of the inexperience of the first sheep farmers, the flocks did well and big profits were made. In December 1849 the farmers could sell a ten-month-old lamb for three guineas ($6.30) each and a breeding ram for twenty guineas ($42). In addition there was money to be made from the sale of the wool fleece. Selling wool was more profitable than growing crops. Soon flocks of sheep, surplus stock from Australia, were being driven inland to find land for grazing. The Canterbury plains seemed especially suitable for sheep. Droughts were not as severe as in Australia, and the rich grasslands provided good feed for the animals. Pastoral farming, that is, sheep grazing, expanded rapidly, especially in the South Island.

A load of wool ready for the market.

The land used by sheep farmers was not then wanted by other farmers. For a small fee they could get a government grazing licence and lease a sheep run of 10,000 acres or more. The hardy merino sheep from Australia flourished on the tussock. Sometimes the farmers would burn the tussock off, so that the sheep could graze on the fresh green shoots of the new growth. No fences were used at first, but instead, shepherds lived in huts on the boundaries to watch for strays.

Mustering sheep. This flock is pictured at the north end of Waihau Beach, travelling south.

Before 1843 there were only a few hundred sheep on Mana Island and in the missionary settlements. Ten years later there were over half a million sheep. After twenty years the number reached three million. Selling wool overseas helped New Zealand prosper.

As sheep farming became more profitable, the demand for land increased and farmers had to search further inland into the rough back country to find unclaimed areas. Sometimes they had to race their rivals to the government office to apply for the grazing licence. Runholders with existing leases bought parts of their runs outright. The runholders were not many in number, but they controlled vast areas of land.

Felling the forest

A timber workers' camp. Notice their saws and axes.

Other settlers earned their living selling timber. The native forest had to be cleared for farming. There was a big demand for timber to build houses, halls, courts and churches for the rapidly increasing population.

Felling the massive kauri and rimu of the North Island forests was hard work. The bushmen worked with axes and crosscut saws. These saws were up to three and a half metres long. In addition, a bushman would have steel wedges, a maul (heavy wooden hammer) and a tin of madoo, a special mix of kerosene and salt-free dripping used to keep the saw blade free of gum. They took great care of their tools. One bushman was heard to boast that he had used the same axe for ten years, though he did admit that it had had three new heads and seven new handles!

When the land was cleared the logs were dragged by bullock teams to sawmills and sawn into planks. Some timber was exported and New Zealand kauri, in particular, was in great demand for shipbuilding. After the 1850s, however, wool was more important than timber for sale overseas.

A side product of the timber industry was the gum secreted by the kauri trees. Maori found that a piece of gum inside a torch of flax leaves bound together burned with a bright light. Settlers in the north collected the gum and used it as a fire-starter. It was also used to make glue, paint and varnish.

Left: Timber worker using a timber 'jack'.

Below: To get the logs down the river valleys to the sawmill, dams were built. This one is ready to trip.

Above: Logs were hauled out of the bush by bullock teams. Getting stuck in the mud was a regular event in the bullocky's day.

Right: Water transport was often the cheapest method to get the timber to the towns. This is the scow Gannet.

A side industry of the timber trade was the collection of kauri gum.

Song of the Gumfield

In the slighted, blighted North where the giant kauris grow,
And the earth is bare and barren where the bush-bee used to hum,
And the luck we've followed's failing and our friends are out of hailing,
And it's getting narrow sailing by the rocks of Kingdom Come,
There's a way of fighting woe, squaring store-bills as you go,
In the trade of digging gum.

And the new chum and the scum
And the scouring of the slum,
And the lawyer and the doctor, and the deaf and halt and dumb,
And the parson and the sailor, and the welsher and the whaler,
When the world is looking glum,
Just to keep from Kingdom Come,
Take to digging kauri gum.

In the scrubby, grubby North when the giddy sun is set,
And the idiot-owl-cicada stops the whirring of his drum;
And the night is growing thicker and the bottled candles flicker,
And the damned mosquitoes bicker in a diabolic hum,
There's a way of ending fret and of pulling down a debt
In the task of scraping gum.

A poem by William Satchell

The gold rushes

It had long been known that there was gold in New Zealand. The vital question was whether there was a field rich enough to be worked. Prospectors explored the remote districts looking for gold. The Otago Provincial Council offered a reward of £500 ($1000) for the discovery of a workable field. Small finds and rumours of gold strikes were not uncommon but it was not until 1861 that the first rush began.

An Australian miner, Gabriel Read, set out to earn the council's reward. He had heard of a find in the Tuapeka area. A miner called Black Peter was rumoured to have found gold at Woolshed Creek. Gabriel Read took a tent, a blanket, a spade, a tin dish, a butcher's knife and a week's supply of provisions. In a gully near Tuapeka (now Lawrence) he finally made a discovery:

> I shovelled away about two and a half feet of gravel, arrived at a beautiful soft slate and saw the gold shining like the stars in Orion on a dark, frosty night.

He worked for ten hours with just his butcher's knife and the tin dish, and in that time panned seven ounces (200 g) of gold. He could have kept the discovery to himself and worked the area secretly, but felt it was his duty to make his find public. He wrote to the Superintendent of Otago and the news was published in the Otago newspaper.

Gold

Bright fine gold.
Bright fine gold.
One a pecker,
Tuapeka,
Bright fine gold.

An Otago goldfields nursery rhyme.

Gabriel's Gully pockmarked with gold miners' claims and their tents.

Staking a claim

At first the people of Dunedin treated it as just another rumour, but within a few weeks the steady stream of miners moving into the Tuapeka area had become a rush. Diggers armed with picks and shovels invaded Gabriel's Gully and a tent town sprang up. By July there were over 11,000 people in the district, nearly all men. They had left their homes and families to chase this new dream. Many came from the Australian goldfields. Sailors jumped ship, soldiers deserted the army — gold fever had hit New Zealand!

When the miners arrived at the field they had to stake out a claim by driving a peg in at each corner. Then they had to register the claim with the officials. Arguments over claims were common and sometimes developed into fights. Miners were always on the alert for news of a fresh field. Sometimes a rumour or even just a miner striding purposefully off into the hills would be enough to start a 'dummy' rush.

In 1862 the news of the discovery of gold around the Clutha River attracted 3,000 men to the diggings at the Dunstan. Then rumours began to spread about a particular miner called William Fox. He came into the Dunstan for supplies, sold quantities of gold and then disappeared into the rugged land of the interior. Could he have discovered a new field? He was watched very carefully when next he came for supplies. A group of miners followed him. He seemed to be very friendly, pitched his tent and shared an evening meal with them. The next morning the tent and the supplies were there, but Fox had gone! Eventually smoke from their cooking fires gave Fox and his companions away. The field on the Arrow River had been found and a new rush was on. Later finds were made in the Shotover River and at Naseby.

This licence, issued for a year, gave the miner the right to work a claim.

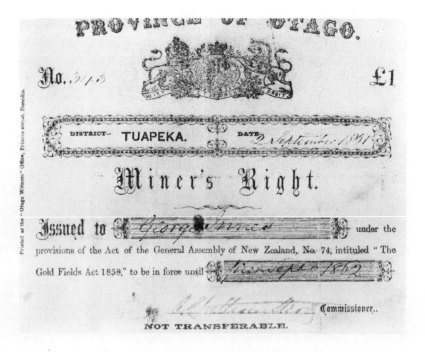

70

Life on the goldfields

The equipment the miners carried was very simple. Their clothes, mining tools such as a tin pan or dish and a pick or spade, a chamois bag in which to hold the gold, were all wrapped lengthwise in a blanket and carried over their shoulders in what was called a 'swag'. They dressed in moleskin trousers, red or grey flannel shirts, a slouch hat called a 'wide-awake', and nugget boots. Their food was plain: mutton bought or stolen from the

Some miners built small shelters or huts to live in while they worked their claims. Notice the shovel and the pan used for separating the gold dust from the tailings.

sheep stations of Central Otago, damper (a mixture of flour and water), and strong tea boiled in a billy. Sometimes they would hunt wild pigs or native birds to add to this diet.

The miners worked long hours panning the gold. On Saturday night they went to the only warm place on the goldfield, the 'pub'. On Sunday they washed their clothes, darned socks and sat around smoking pipes. Hunting and gambling were popular activities, and in Queenstown hard-won gold was wagered on rat fights. Rats were a terrible problem at the diggings, and a small cat was a great treasure for which miners were prepared to pay a high price.

Some miners were lucky and made their fortunes quickly. Two Maori gold miners, Dan Ellison and Hakaria Haeroa, were working in the Shotover River when they saw a beach that looked a good place to pan for gold. Like much of the Shotover, it was difficult to reach. Sheer cliffs, two hundred metres high, forced the pair to swim the river from the opposite side. Other miners did not dare risk the swim because the current was strong and the river cold. Dan and Hakaria crossed successfully, but Dan's pet dog was swept downstream by the current. After the dog managed to scramble ashore on a rocky point, Dan swam down to rescue it. He found that the rocky crevices on the point were filled with

Chinese miners at Tuapeka.
They lived simply in huts
made of slabs of stone.

The miners (or diggers)
and the runholders
(squatters) disliked each
other. The runholders felt
threatened by the swarms
of miners on their land,
stealing their sheep.

coarse gold. He and Hakaria collected 300 ounces (8.5 kg), worth more than £1,200 ($2,400), before nightfall.

Most miners were not so lucky. Panning for gold was not an easy way to earn a living. The gold was hard to find. Living conditions were not just miserable, they were dangerous. Many men were not properly equipped for the harsh Central Otago climate, especially the severe winters. Fuel was so scarce that sometimes miners had to walk twenty kilometres to get enough wood to boil the billy. When the billy boiled, the fire had to be put out to save the sticks for the next time. The miners' boots froze overnight and had to be thawed out under the blankets in the morning. In 1863 nearly 500 men were snowed in without food at a camp high in the hills. Many died trying to walk through the blinding snow and blizzard conditions to the lower camps. For some years later, skeletons found in the hills reminded others of the dangers of seeking gold.

Miners needed to camp close to the rivers to pan the gold. Rivers in flood rose rapidly, sometimes without much warning. Steep valley sides, undermined by the rain, collapsed on top of the miners. In July 1863 heavy rain fell for six days and miners had to retreat to higher ground. Some did not move fast enough and were swept away by flood waters or by slips. People lower down the Clutha saw human bodies, horses and mining equipment bobbing past on the flood waters.

One distinctive group of miners came from China. Wearing their long hair in pigtails, as the Chinese emperor required all Chinese men to do, their belongings carried in baskets slung on long poles, and their large bamboo hats, they looked quite strange to the other miners. They were often treated with suspicion, and were allowed to work only in claims considered worthless. However, they were very hard working and managed to find gold in areas other miners had abandoned. They lived very simply in huts made from slabs of wood or stone, and many returned to China with their savings.

Cromwell had eight or nine hotels, all prospering. None of these had existed eight years before.

Families on the goldfields

There were not many women and children on the early fields, but as small shanty towns developed, more arrived. Women were in great demand. As unmarried women arrived they were met by crowds of miners in their best clothes, hoping for a wife. Most of the women were married within a week. One boasted she had had fifty offers of marriage in one week. The hotel keepers were desperate for barmaids, kitchen-help and dance girls. One hotel keeper asked a friend in Dunedin to send him the ugliest girl he could find. His friend did as the hotel keeper asked. She lasted a fortnight before she too was married.

Living close to the swift-flowing rivers on the goldfields was dangerous for children. There are many reports of children drowning. One story from Arrowtown was more cheerful. Mrs Cotter rushed to rescue her son Tom who was drowning in a waterhole. She was wearing the fashionable crinoline, with a big balloon-like skirt, which must have been most unsuitable for the rough and dangerous living conditions. This time, however, it saved her son's life. The crinoline billowed out and kept his mother afloat long enough for her to drag Tom ashore.

Many young children died from disease. Look at this evidence from the Cromwell graveyard:

Matilda Margaret Scully, Died 30 April 1873, aged 11 months and 23 days
John Scully, Died 27 March 1874, aged 7 years and 3 months
Mary Scully, Died 2 April 1874, aged 5 years and 2 months
Sarah Scully, Died 7 April 1874, aged 6 years and 3 months
Daniel Scully, Died 7 April 1874, aged 3 years and 7 months
Ellen Scully, — their mother, Died 1 April 1875 aged 29 years

The Scully children died during an outbreak of typhoid. Cromwell, like many other towns, drew its water supply from the same area where all the offal and rubbish was thrown.

Hotels on the goldfields made big profits. Some traders or miners made their own drink to sell. This was illegal and the police often made raids to close down these stills. One brand of 'moonshine', Kokatahi whisky, was said to be so strong that it would eat away the bottoms of the tin pannikins used as cups. Gold at the Kumara field on the West Coast was said to have been found when three miners were digging the foundations for an illegal whisky still.

When something unusual happened at the diggings, like a pretty girl visiting, or the police checking that the miners had licences, the miners would call out 'Joe!', and the message would be passed on through the field. All the miners would stop work and stare.

The road to Skippers, near Queenstown, was built by Chinese workers.

With no proper roads, travelling to the goldfields was very difficult. The journey from Dunedin to Tuapeka was 113 kilometres and took seven days. Wagons often stuck fast in the thick mud.

From Tuapeka to the Clutha the road was marked by small saplings that had been planted, each with a small black flag on top. Cairns of rocks marked the road in rocky places. Getting to a claim in the Shotover River could involve a nightmare journey, as the son of a miner describes:

My sister and I were each put in a gin case and these cases were slung across the back of the pony, one on each side. The track was narrow and rough, and the precipices frightfully steep. We were both crying, the men walking in front and behind were swearing and the pony snorted as the boulders rolled over the edge into the abyss below.

A boom time for Dunedin

The ones who prospered from the gold were not the miners. Although a few individuals struck it lucky, most of the miners only made enough to feed themselves and to pay for their heavy drinking sessions. Many lost everything they had in the search for gold.

Camping out on the journey between Christchurch and Hokitika.

The people who made money were those who supplied miners with provisions. They transported food and equipment to the fields to sell at the high prices miners were prepared to pay.

Flour 1s to 3s per lb
Salt 10d per lb or more
Tea 5s to 6s per lb
Butter (salted in kegs) 3s 6d per lb
Sugar 1s 6d per lb
Mutton 1s to 1s 6d per lb
Tobacco 6s per lb
Picks 16s

Buckets £1
Shovels 14s to £1
Bread 4s to 7s for 4 lb loaf
Eggs up to 21s per dozen
Candles (tallow) 1s each
Cartage from Dunedin £130 per ton (about 10 cents per lb for a seven-day trip of 113 km)
Newspapers 2s 6d a copy

At first the people of Dunedin had looked with concern at the rough, brash strangers invading their province. But as Dunedin profited from the huge demand for goods, attitudes changed. Dunedin became the largest town in New Zealand in the 1860s and the most important commercial centre. Banks flourished and industry developed. Waggons, needed to get supplies to the miners, were built in Dunedin. As alluvial or surface gold came to an end and shafts had to be dug, or sluices or dredges built, the need for locally made goods increased.

But gold mining was a short-lived boom. After 1863 the amount of gold from the Otago fields fell sharply and many miners left the area. Some moved to the West Coast of the South Island when gold was found there in 1865–67. Hokitika became a boom town, but it was very difficult to get supplies there. Ships bringing goods by sea came to grief on the dangerous Hokitika bar. Getting stores over the mountains from Christchurch was expensive. On the West Coast fields thick bush, heavy rain and, worst of all, sandflies and mosquitos made gold mining tough work. Men rubbed their faces and hands with bacon to keep the insects off. Frequently men were lost in the bush, or died from starvation. Some drowned in the fast-flowing West Coast rivers.

Getting the gold

A short description of the manner of obtaining gold will be interesting. In some places it is found embedded in hard rock, called quartz; sometimes the gold may be seen in little streaks or veins in the quartz. The quartz is dug out of the ground and carried away to a machine called a battery, composed of heavy stampers, which hammer the quartz until it is reduced to powder — gold and all. During all this time a small stream of water, running through the stampers, washes the powdered quartz and gold through a fine grating.

Underneath the grating is a trough, filled with quicksilver, and next comes a long, broad table covered with copper, intersected with little troughs, upon which quicksilver is laid. Now quicksilver possesses the property of mixing (amalgamating it is called) with gold. Thus, when the flowing water carries the quartz, dust, and gold into the trough of quicksilver, and over the quicksilver-covered table, nearly all the gold is caught by and mixed with the quicksilver. When the crushing has continued for some hours, the stampers are stopped, and all the quicksilver is scraped off the tables and out of the troughs.

This quicksilver contains all the gold that has been washed into it by the action of the water, and the two metals together are called amalgam. The amalgam is then placed in an iron vessel, called the retort, over a fire. When it becomes thoroughly hot the quicksilver evaporates, that is, floats up, and escapes from the retort in the shape of vapour or gas.

This gas is not allowed to escape altogether, for quicksilver is too valuable to be wasted so freely. On the contrary, the gas is conducted through a pipe which leads into a quantity of cold water, thus cooling the gas and causing it to return to quicksilver, its former state. When the heat has caused all the quicksilver to evaporate, the gold remains in a cake at the bottom of the retort; when cold, it is taken out and carried to the Bank.

Above: This is quoted from A Little History of New Zealand ... for Children by E.M. Bourke (1881).

Gold was also found near Thames on the Coromandel coast. However, miners from the West Coast who came to Coromandel in 1867–68 found that there was little surface gold, and expensive machinery was needed to work the quartz reefs.

Gold mining continued on the fields for many years. The easily extracted alluvial gold had gone. Only companies with money to invest could afford the dredges, the sluices and batteries.

Dredging on the Otago rivers and mining in Reefton and Waihi continued, but the big gold boom was over. Only the lonely graves, the deserted shacks and the great heaps of tailings show where thousands of men worked in the hope of striking it rich.

A gold dredge at work.

Extracting gold from the Thames fields required machinery and was too expensive for miners working alone.
This drawing shows Hunt's claim and the Kurunui tramway.

NINE

〜

Wars Between Maori and British, 1860-72

The 1850s were good years for Maori and settlers, but there were still difficulties. Trouble was brewing. Without any doubt its main cause was that in some places the settlers wanted to get land faster than the Maori would sell it. This was especially true in Auckland, where settlers wanted the rich lands of the Waikato, and in Taranaki, where they wanted the Waitara district. Near those two rivers much of the dense bush had long ago been cleared by Maori, so that it would be easy for settlers to cultivate.

For Maori the land was their country; they loved it. To the settlers land meant new farms and profit. They did not yet feel that it was their country. The Maori valued the bush for its birds, berries and other food. The settlers wanted to cut down and burn the bush and plant grass seed. In the end they won, but only after a long and hard struggle.

The Maori had a saying: 'Women and land are the reasons why men die.' This was to prove true in the 1860s. Some of the Maori leaders of earlier days, like Te Rauparaha, had opposed selling land to the government. During the 1850s, as the number of Pakeha increased (passing the Maori population of about 56,000 by 1858), many more Maori came to oppose selling. They wanted to keep plenty of land for nga mokopuna (their grandchildren). Many Taranaki Maori became very determined not to sell. They declared that their land was tapu and not to be sold. Some Maori in southern Taranaki wrote to Robert Parris, a government land purchaser, about their lands: 'These are tapu places, Parris. The guardians of these lands are bush lawyers (vines), nettles, tree ferns; the guardians of the sacred place are reptiles, weta, spiders, taniwha, great lizards.'

Other Maori, however, were keen to sell land and get more money. In some districts, both in Taranaki and Hawke's Bay, there was fighting between the landholders and the landsellers.

The Maori King movement

The settlers had had their own parliament since 1854 and their own government (like the present Cabinet) two years later. Almost no Maori had a vote and there were none in Parliament. Some leading Maori began to aim at uniting the tribes into one people, with its own Maori government. The leader of this movement was a remarkable chief of the Ngatihaua tribe, Wiremu Tamihana (William

Thompson). He was a strong Christian who was devoted to keeping peace between the tribes and between the Pakeha and Maori. In 1858 a large meeting in the Waikato elected a famous old chief, Te Wherowhero, as the first Maori King. He took the name Potatau and soon had his own courts, a flag, troops and constables. He was supported by tribes in the Waikato, Taupo, some from the East Coast, and some from Taranaki. All agreed that their lands were tapu, and put under the king's protection. So the Maori kingdom was a block to Pakeha progress through the centre of the North Island. The Europeans and a large section of the Maori people had set off on different paths. The situation was becoming more dangerous.

Grey's successor as Governor was another army officer, Colonel Gore Browne. He and the government did not understand Maori land customs. They believed that some Maori were ganging up to stop rightful owners of land from selling their own pieces. In

Wiremu Tamihana (William Thompson).

Te Wherowhero, or Potatau, drawn by G.F. Angas.

fact, few if any Maori claimed to own a particular piece of land. Lands were owned in common by the tribe. There were many disputes between different families and sub-tribes or tribes as to who really were the owners. Very often the occupants had changed in recent years.

The Waitara dispute

In 1859 a Maori named Teira (Taylor) offered to sell land at the Waitara River. The great chief Wiremu Kingi (William King) denied that Teira had the right to sell. The chief and a tribe of about 300 people were actually living on the land. Teira and Wiremu Kingi had quarrelled over whether a woman should marry one of Teira's relatives. To get even, Teira offered to sell the land. The government came to the conclusion that Teira and a few of his family owned at least some of the land and determined to accept his offer. The Governor had decided to uphold British law against what he regarded as wrongful interference by Wiremu Kingi. This was a mistake that was to have serious consequences. Only a few years before, in very similar circumstances, a Taranaki Maori had offered to sell disputed land to Governor Grey, who had wisely refused.

Both the Maori and the British were war-like people, who had fought in many battles. The soldier and the warrior alike sought to gain honour in warfare. From now on they did not restrain their anger. The Maori called the New Zealand wars te riri Pakeha (the white man's anger or quarrel) and for many years the Pakeha called them the Maori Wars.

The government bought Teira's land, but when surveyors were sent in, old ladies from Kingi's tribe pulled out their pegs. Kingi built a pa on the land. When the soldiers captured this they found it empty. The local farmers had to retreat into New Plymouth while the Maori burned farmhouses. Large numbers of Maori from south Taranaki, and from the Waikato and Ngati Maniapoto tribes, came to help Kingi.

Eventually there were about 3,000 European troops fighting some 1,500 Maori. Though they were outnumbered, the Maori did well in the fighting. They would build a pa that was very strong but did not protect anything very important. They would make sure that it had a good escape route, such as a bush-covered gully, nearby. If a medium-sized British force attacked, it would be beaten. If the British went to the trouble of getting together a big force, the Maori would simply leave. However, this clever system of war did not always work. The British were able to keep hold of Waitara. Once they caught some Waikato Maori in an unfinished pa and killed most of them. But the Maori burned the settlers' houses around New Plymouth and seized a block of British land in revenge for the loss of Waitara. So the first war was a kind of draw and the settlers were not very happy with their British generals, Gold and Pratt. One settler wrote a nursery rhyme about them:

General Gold
Was not very old;
General Pratt
Was not very fat;
But all the motions of General Gold
Were as slow as if he'd been fat and old;
And all the motions of General Pratt
Were as slow as if he'd been old and fat.

Wiremu Kingi.

In 1861, through the help of Wiremu Tamihana, a truce was arranged. But no one believed that the fighting was over. Wiremu Kingi and his warriors retreated to the Waikato. It was there, it seemed, in the Maori King's lands, that the main battles would be fought.

Governor Grey returns

This was a time of wild rumours among both the Maori and the Pakeha: stories of imminent attack on the settlers; fear that the government was going to take Maori land. Many people were frightened. Governor Gore Browne was preparing to invade the Waikato to put down the Maori King, but the British government did not approve. He was sacked and Sir George Grey was brought back as governor again to see what he could do.

Grey did introduce some good measures in the Maori districts, hoping that the Maori would treat him as their father, but the 'King' Maori did not trust him and they may have been right. Grey thought that the existence of the

Maori King threatened the rule of Queen Victoria. He built a military road pointing straight down the Waikato valley.

In southern Taranaki, hostile Maori had taken some European land. They said that if the troops tried to get it back they would 'fight for New Zealand to the death'. (Similarly, Wiremu Kingi had written in 1860, 'What though my people and I may die, we die for New Zealand.') Such remarks show that for the Maori, this was their country.

War in the Waikato

Grey sent troops to take that land. Rewi Maniapoto, a great chief of the Ngati Maniapoto tribe, who lived near Te Kuiti, wrote advising the Taranaki Maori to attack. They ambushed some soldiers and war began again. After inflicting a defeat on the Taranaki Maori the British army, led by General Duncan Cameron, invaded the Waikato. By 1864 there were 12,000 British and colonial troops as well as a thousand Maori allies fighting against the Maori King party and their allies, who numbered perhaps 4,000. These numbers may seem small compared to modern wars, but we must remember that the whole Maori population was very small. To the King Maori, an attack by 12,000 men was like an attack by a million men on New Zealand today.

During the fighting in 1863–64 the Maori earned a reputation among the British army as being among the most formidable enemies they had ever fought. One soldier who fought against them wrote, 'If they had the same weapons as the British they would make it very warm for troops under General Cameron.' In fact they did make it hot for the British.

The Maori tried to stop the huge British army by building big pa or groups of pa

along its line of advance. When you drive along the main road south from Auckland you can see the sites of two of these pa — Meremere and Rangiriri. The Maori strategy was good, but the trouble was that their soldiers could only fight part time, while the British fought full time. Maori warriors had to visit home after a few weeks' campaigning to check on their families, get more supplies, and help grow food. So their 4,000 men were never in the field at the same time, and there were periods when they did not have enough warriors to hold their big pa. This is just what happened at the battle of Rangiriri. Here 183 Maori surrendered, but only after they had driven off no less than seven British attacks and killed and wounded 132 soldiers. General Cameron now turned his attack against the Ngati Maniapoto tribe. Some of them, led by Rewi Maniapoto, built a pa in a grove of peach trees at Orakau, which was soon surrounded by British troops. There were about 300 Maori from several tribes, including women and children. The British and colonial troops numbered about 2,000.

The Maori fortifications at Rangiriri, 1863, with soldiers standing about after the battle.

Rewi Maniapoto.

For three days the Maori resisted bayonet charges and artillery fire. In the end they had nothing to eat but raw potatoes, and nothing to fire but wooden bullets. The general called upon them to surrender. Rewi replied, 'Ka whawhai tonu ake! Ake! Ake!' (We will fight on forever, forever, forever!) There were many Maori women in the pa, and they refused the General's offer to allow them to leave. Some of these women were later killed.

Suddenly the Maori walked out in a body towards some of the soldiers. For a moment the troops did not realise what was happening. About 150 Maori, including Rewi, escaped into the swamps, though many died. The defence of Orakau was a defeat that was a kind of victory. General Cameron wrote:

> One cannot help admiring the heroism of these Maori in holding out so bravely against such immense odds, and then preferring to try to force their way out, with almost certain prospect of death, rather than surrender.

In the church at Te Awamutu the troops erected a tablet in memory of the Maori killed at Orakau and another battle. It said, 'I say unto you, love your enemies.' This remarkable memorial shows how much the soldiers respected their foe.

The battle of Gate Pa

General Cameron now turned his attention to beating the Maori near Tauranga. The Ngai te Rangi built a pa called Gate Pa close to the soldiers' camp. About 1,650 troops, including the 'crack' 43rd Regiment, attacked about 250 Maori, including a woman, Heni Te Kiri-Karamu, who stayed to fight alongside her brother when the other women were sent to villages in the rear. She refused to obey a chief's order for her to leave, saying:

The army attacks Nukumaru Pa, 1865.

I shall not leave this pa unless my brother leaves also. If it is right that he should stay then I am his equal; I can use a gun and I shall stay.

A detachment of Armed Constabulary in Tauranga during the late 1860s.

The battle opened with a very heavy barrage of shells from the big guns. Each shell from the biggest gun weighed fifty kilograms. The British soldiers were sure no one could have survived the heavy pounding. The soldiers and sailors charged the pa with their bayonets ready to kill any survivors. But the Ngai te Rangi had become experts at building trenches and covered pits like those used in the much later First World War. They had sheltered from the barrage and were ready to counterattack. The British troops were completely taken by surprise when, from under their feet, the Maori guns blazed. For the British the attack was a disaster — 112 men were dead or wounded. The rest fled in disarray. The Maori treated the wounded with much kindness. Heni took water to a dying British colonel.

The British took revenge soon after, when they caught the local Maori in an unfinished pa at Te Ranga. About a hundred Maori were killed and wounded during a bayonet charge. The Arawa tribe from Rotorua were successful allies of the British. They defeated the Maori King's supporters on the East Coast.

The British now took large areas of Maori land in the Waikato and Taranaki, near Tauranga and elsewhere. The government settled former soldiers on some of this land, hoping to make the towns more secure from attack. The Maori never forgave this confiscation of land. It went quite against the Treaty of Waitangi.

It might have seemed in 1864 that the war was over. In fact it was to go on for another eight years, and the fighting became increasingly bitter.

The Hau-hau

Shortly after the battle of Orakau, British soldiers in Taranaki were attacked by a group of Maori who shouted 'Hau! Hau!' during the skirmish. The Hau-hau, as they came to be called, belonged to a new religious group — the Pai Marire (Good and Peaceful) religion. This had been started by Te Ua, who had seen the Angel Gabriel in a vision. His followers believed that if they shouted 'Pai marire! Hau! Hau!' they would be safe from Pakeha bullets. Of course they were not, but many of them showed incredible bravery in battle.

One of the Hau-hau chiefs, Titokowaru, won a series of victories against the colonial troops. On a few occasions the Hau-hau revived the custom of cannibalism, which both disgusted and frightened the settlers. Titokowaru was a brilliant general and for a time reconquered most of the land between Mount Egmont and Wanganui. At one time, fear of Titokowaru was so great that the settlers abandoned Palmerston North and called out the militia in Wellington and the Hutt Valley. Titokowaru was never defeated in battle, but for some mysterious reason his followers left him in 1869 and he could fight no longer.

Below: This is quoted from **A Little History of** New Zealand ... **for Children by** *E.M. Bourke (1881).*

A Hau-hau attack

A party of Hau-haus went to Captain Wilson's house, where he lived with his wife and nine children. He endeavoured to defend his house for some time, but at last it was set on fire by the Maoris, and he was obliged to leave it. The Maoris promised to spare the lives of his family on condition that he would hand over his firearms; so relying on this, he came out, carrying his little boy on his back, his other children, with Mrs Wilson, following. When a little way from the house the Maoris murdered them all, except the little boy, who, falling underneath his father's body, was not noticed in the confusion.

Mrs Wilson was wounded and left for dead. The murderers went from house to house, killing all they met, and many narrow escapes are related. A monument stands in the cemetery, three miles from Gisborne, on which the names and ages of the victims are inscribed . . .

This boy was only seven years of age, and when his father was killed, being frightened, he remained quiet until the Hau-haus had gone on; he then stole away into the scrub and hid himself; next day he came out, and, looking about, found his mother sadly wounded, but alive. She had crawled into the out-house. For seven days this poor woman had lived there until help came; her little boy brought her water, and found eggs enough for both. When found by the Volunteers she was taken carefully to Gisborne, after which she was removed to Napier, where she died within a few weeks.

Te Kooti

The Hau-hau religion spread into the Waikato, Hawke's Bay and the East Coast, and soon the British had another foe, as dangerous as Titokowaru. During the fighting on the East Coast a Maori named Te Kooti, who was fighting on the side of the British, was arrested and accused of being in touch with the Hau-

Hau-hau prisoners captured at Weraroa Pa, 1865, and imprisoned in the Rutland stockade at Wanganui. Notice the girl at the right.

hau. This he denied and always said that he was a 'Queen's Maori'. Te Kooti wrote three letters demanding a proper trial, but he was shipped off to the Chatham Islands without a hearing. There he studied the Bible and started a new religion, Ringatu (the Upraised Hand).

In 1868 Te Kooti and his friends seized a schooner and escaped back to New Zealand. Here he proved a dangerous guerrilla fighter and enemy of the settlers. He engaged in many actions. He and his men attacked and killed many of the settlers and 'friendly' Maori at Poverty Bay. His Maori enemies later took revenge by shooting some of his followers after taking them prisoner. Te Kooti fought in many battles. He did not win them all, but he never gave in.

Perhaps a thousand men were killed in battle on each side during the wars, and some civilians were killed in raids or died of starvation. Large areas of Maori land had been taken as punishment. The Maori King and his allies continued to stop European settlers from entering the 'King Country'. But, in the long run, they ceased to block settlement and by the early 1880s began to sell land again.

The kainga (village) at Parihaka, 1881. Te Whiti's house is said to be at the back on the left. Notice the mixture of Maori whare, European houses — and a tent.

The Charge of Parihaka

Yet a league, yet a league,
Yet a league onward,
Straight to the Maori pah
Marches the Twelve
  Hundred.
'Forward the Volunteers!
Is there a man who fears!'
Over the ferny plain
Marched the Twelve
  Hundred.

Children to right of them,
Children to left of them,
Women in front of them,
Saw them and wondered,
Stormed at with jeer and
  groan,
Foiled by the five alone,
Never was trumpet blown
O'er such a deed of arms
Back with their captives
  three,
Taken so gallantly,
Rode the Twelve Hundred.

When can their glory fade!
Oh! The wild charge they
  made!
New Zealand wondered
Whether each doughty soul
Paid for the pigs he stole,
Noble Twelve Hundred!

A poem by Jessie Mackay.

Parihaka

There were no more wars in New Zealand, but there were still areas where Maori rejected Pakeha authority. In the centre of the North Island the King Movement held up settlement. In southern Taranaki a new Maori prophet, Te Whiti, foretold the day when the Pakeha would all go and leave New Zealand for the Maori. Te Whiti opposed drinking alcohol and the prayer meetings he conducted in his village at Parihaka attracted many followers.

Te Whiti believed that his tribe had been promised reserves when the government had taken their land. These had not been given. To the Maori, of course, it was their land, not government land. Te Whiti's followers began to resist government attempts to settle Pakeha on confiscated land. They pulled out survey pegs and ploughed up nearby European farms in a non-violent protest. What scared the government was that a leader of the ploughing parties was the famous guerrilla fighter Titokowaru.

In 1881 the Native Minister, John Bryce, led an expedition of 1,600 troops to occupy Parihaka, where they were met by a couple of hundred children, singing and dancing. One of our early poets, Jessie Mackay, wrote a parody of 'The Charge of the Light Brigade' to celebrate the victory of the militia.

Te Whiti and another leader, Tohu, were arrested and locked up for a year. When they went back Te Whiti built a model village with piped water and electricity. This was a new effort to lead his people to a successful life in the world of the Pakeha. Other efforts were to come.

TEN

Family Life in the Late Nineteenth Century

The 1860s had been the time of wars and gold. By the end of the sixties the wars were almost over and the gold was running out. Men who had come to New Zealand to look for gold or make a profit from goldfields trade began to drift away again. Pakeha New Zealand was a string of settlements around the edges of the two main islands. They were isolated from one another, fiercely competitive, and suspicious of one another. The South Island provinces were quite rich because of income from wool and gold. The North Island provinces, especially Taranaki, had suffered from the wars. Gloom descended as people began to fear that the hopes of the early settlers would never be fulfilled. New Zealand would not be the garden of the Pacific: she would not be a land of milk and honey nor of golden opportunity. People started to move away. They went to Australia or off to seek their fortunes in California.

Sir Julius Vogel

At this time of uncertainty and disappointment one man came forward with an idea. The pattern of New Zealand's development has been that times of growth and change have been followed by times of uncertainty and confusion, sometimes despair; then some new idea will be suggested that gets the country moving again, often in a new direction. The man who seemed to have the answers to the problems of the 1870s was Julius Vogel. Vogel was an adventurer who had gone from England to work on the Australian goldfields as a gold assayer when he was only seventeen. In 1861 he followed the gold-seekers to Otago, working as a newspaper reporter. In November of that year he had helped to found New Zealand's first daily paper, the *Otago Daily Times*. Vogel was elected to Parliament in 1863 and in 1869 he became Colonial Treasurer (Minister of Finance).

A portrait of Sir Julius Vogel drawn for the Christchurch Illustrated Press *in 1873.*

Borrowing for growth

Vogel's 1870 Budget was a bombshell. He startled Parliament by suggesting that the central government borrow £6 million ($12 million) over the next ten years to meet the chief needs of the country — roads, railways and immigrants. Money had been borrowed before, but never so much for so long, or to carry out such a definite plan of development. Vogel seemed to be a financial genius. His policies would bring thousands of new people to New Zealand. Growth would begin again. Moreover, it would be more co-operative, better-planned growth. The roads and railways that Vogel planned would draw the scattered provinces together. Before 1870 it was often easier to go from Auckland to Sydney than from Auckland to Wellington. There were no roads through the centre of the North Island. People travelled by coastal ships and by horseback on rough bush tracks. Railway lines were disconnected fragments reaching inland from ports. In 1874 there were only 418 kilometres of railway tracks in the whole country.

The uncomfortable side of travel by coastal shipping. This sketch is from the Christchurch Illustrated Press of 1872.

The new immigrants

Over a hundred thousand people, many of them children, came to New Zealand in the 1870s on immigration schemes. It was the first time a really large number of families had come here. Our first settlers were adventurers, mostly single men —

whalers, sealers, seamen. The missionaries and the settlers of the 1840s and 1850s had brought families, but the people who came in the 1860s were mostly single men once more — miners, storekeepers and soldiers. Many of these people had moved on again fairly quickly and their long-term effect on our history was slight. The children who came in the 1870s were our most valuable immigrants. They stayed. Their families worked on the last and hardest of the pioneering tasks of the nineteenth century — clearing the heaviest of the North Island forests. These immigrants built the roads and railways that joined a collection of provinces into one country.

Cleared land is fenced to make farms at Pakuratahi, north of Featherston. Burned logs and stumps can be clearly seen. Trees that have been killed but not consumed by the fire still stand in the paddocks.

By 1870 the easiest land had already been taken up for farming. The grassy plains of the South Island and the open country in the North Island were used for sheep farming. The forest on the volcanic soil of the Waikato and Taranaki was already being cleared.

The dense forest of the lower North Island was an even more difficult task. Here the soil was heavier. The undergrowth was more dense and the trees, chiefly rimu and totara, were huge. They were up to twenty-five metres high and two metres thick. Fires would kill these giants but not consume them. They had to be cut down by hand with axes and saws. Some of the timber was used for building, but much of it was wasted. It was a careless way to treat trees that had taken hundreds of years to grow; but to people of that time the forest was not a store of timber to be treasured, it was an enemy. The trees stood in the way of farms and roads, so they were destroyed.

91

A home in the bush

The families brought in to clear the North Island forest came from Scandinavia. The government thought that they would be used to forest work, but they had never seen forests as dense as those of the lower North Island. Many of them were farmers who were not skilled at tree felling. As each group arrived in New Zealand it was taken into the bush and shown the area to be cleared. The idea was that they would hack their way towards each other along the road and rail routes. Then they could clear the forty-acre (sixteen hectare) blocks of land granted to each family.

The families who did this work were mostly young and poor. They had agreed to come to New Zealand because they had been promised farms. They had been told that the land had trees on it which they would have to cut down before they could start farming. But it was not possible for anyone in nineteenth-century Europe to imagine what New Zealand's forest was like. It was utterly strange to them. They were afraid of the bush, of its thick undergrowth and the isolation of their settlements. They suffered great hardship. Most knew little or no English. Their wages on the road and railway projects were only fifty cents a day. The cost of their fares from Europe and their transport to the bush sites was deducted from their pay. Nevertheless they did the work they had agreed to do.

When families arrived in the bush the first job was to build a rough hut out of timber slabs or ponga logs. Everyone helped. The usual plan was a two-roomed hut with a door in the middle and a window on each side — like a small child's drawing of a house. There was no glass. The windows were filled in with oiled cloth. The roof was thatched with ponga and fern. One room was used as a bedroom for the whole family. The other, which had a fireplace at one end, was the kitchen. The floor was stamped-down earth.

After the hut was built no time was wasted in attacking the bush. The men chopped down the big trees while women and children cleared smaller trees and undergrowth. They also gathered food from the forest: eels, fat pigeons, wild honey and weka eggs. The men hunted wild pigs. There were no schools to go to at this time. No one had time to spare for anything but clearing the bush. When that was out of the way they could start their farms.

The trees were too damp to burn until they had been cut down and left for three or four months to dry. Sometimes the fires got out of control. In 1888 a big fire destroyed thirty homes and almost wiped out the town of Norsewood. When a burn was successful it got rid of all the cut bush, leaving only the monstrous stumps in the ground. The ash made a useful fertiliser and grass would be sown in place of the trees. Cattle could graze among the stumps. The last job was digging out and burning the stumps. That needed draught horses or bullock teams, and neighbours helped each other until it was done.

When the land was cleared the settlers grew wheat. Sometimes they took the grain to the nearest town to be ground into flour, but many families ground it themselves in a hand mill. Grinding was often a job for children. It took two

hours every day to make enough flour for an average family's bread. As well as growing their own food, the bush farms kept sheep for homespun wool. The women and girls made butter, which could not always be sold for cash but most stores would take it in exchange for other goods.

Life in the bush settlements was much harder than most twentieth-century New Zealanders have known. There were no luxuries. It was scary, lonely and dangerous. Small children sometimes wandered away and were never found. The compensation was that everyone was working hard to improve the family's life. The work of even quite young children was valuable. And the settlers' lives did improve, for the most part. Small farms replaced the huts in the forest clearings. Roads replaced bush tracks. Children went to school. By the end of the nineteenth century the farmhouses were regularly visited by a fascinating procession of travelling salesmen. Dentists, tailors, watch-menders, piano tuners, tinkers, photographers brought their skills and their goods to the back door. Life was more varied and much more comfortable than it had been in the ponga hut with the dirt floor.

The Short family and their bush farmhouse at Coromandel. The wooden chimney is built well out from the thatch because of fire risk. In front of the house camp ovens and a tin bath can be seen amongst the logs. Although the home is very rough, Mrs Short has lace curtains for her windows. The pinafores are dazzlingly white.

93

Pioneer children

There were a lot of children in New Zealand after the family migration of the 1870s. Also, New Zealand was a healthy place to bring up families. Families tended to be large because more healthy babies were born and more of them lived to grow up than in Europe. This was especially true in the country areas. In 1881 forty-two percent of New Zealand people were younger than fifteen. They were children of parents who had come to a new country in the hope of a better life. For most of the parents that hope included better chances for their children. They were quick to build schools in the new settlements. Primary education did not become compulsory until 1877, but before that most New Zealand children were learning to read and write, even if their parents could not. Education was easier to get in the towns, but small schools were set up in country areas as soon as the first frantic stage of pioneering was over. In Maori communities, parents provided the land and contributed towards the teacher's salary. The government paid the rest. The teaching was in English and the teacher was usually Pakeha. By 1879 there were 57 of these schools set up.

Children in New Zealand, even in poor families, had more to eat than most children in Europe. There was plenty of meat, cheese, bread and milk. Butchers gave away scrap meat for dogs and cats. Working-class families in nineteenth-century England ate meat only once or twice a week and rarely saw milk.

Most children in nineteenth-century New Zealand were

One of the large families of the 1870s. Mr and Mrs Thomas Roots and their twelve children in front of their home at Springvale. This photograph was taken by the Wanganui photographer W.J. Harding.

expected to work. Homes were usually smaller and less comfortable than the houses we live in. Families were larger. There were very few labour-saving gadgets. Those that did exist would seem very cumbersome and hard to manage to us now. Try to visit a local historical museum and look at an early washing machine, or a butter churn, or a corn husker, or a mangle. They were not run by electricity. They were made of heavy metal and used human energy to turn their wheels. Household chores were done by women and children. Richer houses employed extra help.

A teenage girl sets off on her mail run from Paranui to Mangonui, near Doubtless Bay in Northland.

Rosamond Rolleston describes the mountains of hand sewing that her grandmother's household achieved. They made shirts, all the children's clothes, riding habits and dresses of all kinds, chair covers, curtains, pillows, even a tent. Relatives' needs were added to the list: 'Finished six nightgowns for the Ormond cousins. . . I made four pairs of drawers [knickers] for Mrs Ormond, two frocks and four pairs of drawers for Harriet.'

Girls went to work as household help when they were about eleven or twelve. Many boys got jobs on farms or factories at about the same age. Joseph Ward, who was later Prime Minister, started work as a telegram delivery boy in the Bluff Post Office when he was twelve. That was in 1869. In 1873 he was sacked

for giving cheek to the postmaster. In 1872 a twelve-year-old girl called Christina McIlvride was employed to collect the mails for her parents who ran the Wainuiomata Post Office. Wainuiomata was then an isolated settlement. To collect the mail she had to ride fifteen kilometres on horseback over a rough hill road to Lower Hutt. She made the thirty-kilometre round trip twice a week for seven years, until she married and left home.

Travellers from Europe often commented on how independent New Zealand children were. Edward Wakefield said that 'they learn to help themselves, in all sorts of ways, at an age when children in England are still quite helpless, or at least in pretty tight leading-strings. Their parents encourage them to help themselves, and are proud of their independence.' They were accustomed to real work at an early age. They also faced real dangers on their long treks to school. Probably most of them were less supervised in their free time than twentieth-century children are. Long working hours for men and time-consuming household work for women gave parents very little time to keep an eye on their older children. They often ran a little wild.

Toys and games

In their free time nineteenth-century children amused themselves in a lot of different ways. They had toys — spinning tops, hoops, dolls, dolls' prams and dolls' houses. Some of these were very elaborate and beautiful. Mechanical wind-up toys made of painted tin were popular. Girls had china-headed dolls with jointed arms and legs and beautifully made clothes.

A kind of bicycle called the velocipede was invented in the 1860s, but it was heavy, uncomfortably bumpy, and slow. The invention of the so-called 'safety bicycle' in the 1880s was a real breakthrough with its light wheels and front-wheel steering. In 1888 pneumatic tyres and the diamond frame were added, creating a safe, cheap and comfortable bike. It was also fast. A bicycle rider could cover 80 to 120 kilometres a day easily — and a bike, unlike a horse, needed no food or water. They became extraordinarily popular; bicycling was a world-wide mania in the 1890s. Then, as cars became more available after the First World War, adults turned to them. Bicycles, however, are still a major pleasure for young people.

Party games — blind man's buff, hunt-the-slipper and treasure hunts — were much the same then as they are now. Children of that time also played some of the same playground games as we do: hopscotch, marbles and ball games. Some playground games were much rougher than modern schools would allow — especially tag games like 'bar-the-door' and battle games.

Rules of team games were not firmly fixed. In any case children made rules to suit themselves. Rounders and tennis were popular. A game called 'tip cat' was played instead of cricket. The 'cat' was a stick fifteen centimetres long and pointed at both

Mary Elizabeth Darrow and her brothers, George and Alec, with their new bicycles. This photograph was taken at Thames about 1895, at the height of the bicycle craze.

The Mt Albert Literary Society on a picnic outing to the Waitakeres in 1904.

ends. The aim was to see who could hit the 'cat' farthest. Rugby was first played in Nelson in the 1870s. Matches would be held with twenty, thirty, even forty players a side and went on as long as people wanted to play; often they lasted all day.

Crazes took hold and vanished just as suddenly then as they do now. Here is part of a letter from Maurice Richmond, aged thirteen, to his cousin Richard Richmond, written in 1873.

An Australian firm advertises musical instruments in the Christchurch Press *in January 1869.*

There have been two or three circuses here a little while ago, and nearly every boy in Nelson practises on single trapezes, treble trapezes and horizontal bars. . . But now we are getting tired of gymnastics, and we play hockey at the college now. Hockey is a game with sticks like walking sticks and a ball, and you have to hit the ball through goals. You very often get hurt in hockey and a good many boys have got black eyes and hurts in other places. . .

People also joined in large organised gatherings such as sports days and picnics. There would be bands and sports competitions. Regattas were popular, but they were for all sorts of boats as well as yachts. There were always big community picnics on New Year's Day.

As homes grew more comfortable it was possible to use them for pleasure as well as eating and sleeping. Families entertained one another. Many girls learned to play the piano. Even in quite isolated places time would be found for girls to take lessons, even if it meant riding some distance on horseback to get to a teacher. In 1901 there were 1,400 music teachers in New Zealand and probably 43,000 pianos. The total population at this time was less than 800,000.

The Tarawera eruption

At three o'clock in the morning of 10 June 1886 Henry Roche, the foreman of a team of surveyors working on a railway line near Rotorua, was sitting in his tent watching the eruption of New Zealand's newest volcano. He saw showers of red-hot scoria thrown into the air and pieces of rock 'as big as houses' shining white with the heat.

> The light in the sky resembled the glow from a great fire, and the eruption . . . began to spread along the top of the mountain until the whole length was in action. The whole mountain appeared to crack open, and its crest became red hot. We then beheld the striking spectacle of a dark, flat-topped mountain more than a mile long, red-hot along its crest, and surmounted by a wall of fire 1,500 feet high. Over this hung . . . dense black smoke clouds through which the forked lightning flashed without ceasing.

The eruption was heard as far away as Christchurch. It rattled windows in Blenheim and Nelson. In Auckland the volcanic explosions sounded like continuous artillery fire and the flashes were mistaken for a gun battle at sea, maybe with a Russian warship. The *Herald* reported that morning that the 'flash of

The great rift blasted in the top of Mt Tarawera by the eruption.

RUINS OF HASZARDS HOUSE.

The ruins of the Haszard family's house.

guns firing was plainly visible from the cupola of the *Herald* office'. Closer to the volcano, frightened people described it as 'a prolonged roar'.

Tarawera was some distance from the volcanoes known to be active, and it blew without any warning that local people could have recognised. The closest people to Tarawera lived in the Maori village of Te Wairoa and at the nearby Terrace Hotel, built for tourists visiting the famous Pink and White Terraces of Rotomahana. Sixty-five of the seventy homes at Te Wairoa were destroyed and eleven people in that village were killed. Other villages nearby — Tokiniho, Moura, Rotomahana, Waingongoro and Totariki — were swept away altogether. There were no survivors and the land was so completely changed by the volcano that no bodies were ever found. Over 100 Maori and seven Pakeha died. Starving horses, cattle and pigs roamed over the ash-covered land but there was no one to feed them. Charles Haszard, the school teacher at Te Wairoa, and four children died when their house collapsed under a rain of volcanic mud. His wife Amelia was rescued the next day after seven hours buried in her collapsed living room cradling a smothered child. Two older daughters also survived. Later Amelia was offered a new job at another school at Te Waotu, where she started teaching on 1 November. The famous Pink and White Terraces were utterly destroyed in the eruption.

The ghost canoe

Rawiri outside his buried whare at Te Wairoa after the eruption.

On 1 June, a week before the eruption, a party of Maori and tourists who were out on the lake with Guide Sophia saw a large waka or war canoe travelling very fast towards Mount Tarawera. The paddlers were completely silent, taking no notice of the calls and shouts of the Maori in Guide Sophia's party. When the tourists later asked about the mysterious canoe they were told that no such waka existed on the lake. Later it was described as a 'phantom canoe'; a ghostly warning of the disaster about to happen.

ELEVEN

Many Settlements Become One

Times were hard in the 1880s. Vogel's loan money had not saved New Zealand from the effects of the worldwide depression. Overseas prices for wool, New Zealand's main export, were low. The new industries in the towns could not provide enough jobs for those who needed to work. Men tramped from farm to farm looking for odd jobs. Many people left New Zealand to settle in Australia. Those who stayed wanted to farm on their own land. This was difficult because much of the cleared land was divided into huge sheep-runs. Sheep farmers were waiting until prices improved before they could sell their land. Settlers looked longingly at Maori land.

A depression is a time when it is very difficult to sell exports overseas. From the late 1870s to 1895 New Zealand's economy was not developing. Low prices for exports made it difficult to pay for all the imports New Zealand needed. Businesses collapsed. Farmers had no money to improve their farms or to develop new agricultural products. Some farmers lost their farms because they could not pay their mortgage repayments. Many men were out of work. Their families were poorly housed and badly fed because there was no government provision for the unemployed.

Bad working conditions

In towns even those with jobs were suffering. Workers in factories, particularly in the clothing industry, worked long hours. Young children had to work because their parents needed the money they earned to help feed the family. Sometimes the children earned the only money the family had. Factories were often overcrowded, poorly lit and stuffy. Machinery did not have safety guards. Pay was low. In Dunedin a Presbyterian minister, the Reverend Rutherford Waddell, was very shocked by the working conditions of clothing workers. In 1888 the

The Sweater

Who robs the widow of her rights,
By work that takes her day and night,
To earn her poor starvation mite?
The Sweater.

Who is it makes girls go astray,
To earn their bread in sinful way,
Because for work he will not pay?
The Sweater.

Who is it that will cheat and lie,
And every cunning trick will try,
His greed of gain to satisfy?
The Sweater.

Who is the vilest, meanest thief,
That trades in flesh and blood and grief,
Till from his fangs death brings relief?
The Sweater.

Who has the rings and jewels on,
And gloats o'er money he has won,
By dirty business he has done?
The Sweater.

He is society's disgrace,
And must be told so to his face;
So out with him, leave him no place,
The Sweater.

A poem from the *Lyttelton Times* of 23 March 1884.

Otago Daily Times printed his sermon 'The Sin of Cheapness'. A special commission was set up to investigate his claims. People were horrified to find that boys and girls could be hired for seventy-five cents a week or less. Some were paid nothing for the first year because the employer said they were 'being trained'. Some girl apprentices had worked for twelve months for no wages and had then been fired. People worked in crowded conditions. In one case seven women were working in a cellar measuring 3.6 by 2.4 by 2.4 metres. In another case, fourteen young girls were working in a room 6.4 by 3.4 by 2.6 metres.

Factory workers in a Dunedin woollen mill.

Outworkers who finished shirts and trousers at home were very poorly paid. One woman, with two tiny children to look after, worked at finishing shirts all day, sometimes until 11.00 p.m. She earned four cents a day. Even those who considered themselves well treated worked very long hours. One worker described the conditions:

> I am a cook in a sixpenny eating-house at the Railway Dining-rooms. I have to get my fire alight by six o'clock in the morning and work till seven in the evening. No meal-hours are allowed. I get my food as I can. I get an hour to myself in the afternoon. I have no complaint to make about my kitchen. My experience of other places is worse. I have worked from five or six in the morning till ten at night. My wages are 12s a week, as I have only just left the Hospital, and am rheumatic. The average of other places is 15s to £1. A housemaid would earn 13s working about the same hours. The charges are 9d for bed and 6d for meals. . . I do not complain so much about myself, as I think I am well treated, but I have come forward to give confidence to others who are in a far worse condition than myself.

The Dunedin took the first shipment of frozen meat to England in 1882.

However, there were developments which, in time, would help New Zealanders earn more money overseas. In 1882 the first cargo of frozen meat left Port Chalmers on the ship *Dunedin* bound for Britain. The *Dunedin* was a fast, iron-hulled sailing ship, fitted with insulated meat chambers, boilers and freezing machinery. Cinders from the boilers kept burning holes in the sails and the captain feared that the masts would burn down. The trip took ninety-eight days and the cargo of meat reached Britain in good condition. The meat sold at a good price — sixpence ha'penny a pound (sixteen cents a kilogram).

There were other technological changes which were to help New Zealanders prosper. Railway building, the telegraph, and later the telephone network were to make it easier to transport goods, to travel and to keep in touch with one another.

However, it was to be another ten years before these changes would improve the living standards of most New Zealanders. What was to be done about economic problems in the meantime? This was the main issue before voters in the 1890 election. Two possibilities were put before them.

The Liberal Party, led by John Ballance, believed that government should try to change society to help all citizens have a better life. Other politicians believed that in time the economy would right itself and that government should interfere as little as possible. The Liberals won the election, and John Ballance became the new Prime Minister.

The Liberal Government

Between 1891 and 1895, the Liberal Government passed a series of laws to improve the lives of New Zealanders. To help families get farms, the government bought large blocks of land, like the Cheviot Estate in North Canterbury. Eighty people lived on this huge sheep station. Its 34,000 hectares were divided into small farms and 650 new settlers moved in. A small town was built where only sheep had grazed.

Even when a family had obtained land to farm, the first five years were very difficult. Sometimes it had to be cleared, a house built and stock purchased. There would be very little income until the land was productive. To help farmers the government lent them money at low rates of interest.

Overseas prices for farm products began to rise. Frozen meat and, later, dairy products were selling well in Britain. Small family farms became profitable and country towns began to flourish. Every district now had a school, even if children had to ride their horses over rough tracks to get there. County councils had begun to improve the roads, and district halls and libraries were built as new communities became more established.

Conditions in factories improved. William Pember Reeves, the Minister of Labour, made new laws. There were to be strict regulations for ventilation, space and working hours. No boy or girl under fourteen years old was to work in a factory. Boys under sixteen years and all women and girls were not permitted to work more than forty-eight hours a week. Their hours of work were to be between 7.45 a.m. and 6.00 p.m. Inspectors were appointed to make sure that these laws were obeyed.

John Ballance, Leader of the Liberal Party, which became the government in 1891.

To prevent strikes, Reeves set up a new system for fixing wages and working conditions. Workers and employers had to take their arguments to a committee for discussion and compromise. If this did not succeed, both the workers and employers had to appear before a special court called the Arbitration Court. A judge would listen to both sides of the argument and make a decision that both workers and employers would have to accept. For the first ten years the system worked very well. New Zealand became famous as the 'land without strikes'. In later years the workers began to feel that the court sided with the

Bell's Match Factory, Wellington.

employers too often. By 1908 some unions were beginning to use strikes, which were occasionally against the law. In 1912 there was a long and bitter miners' strike in Waihi. Industrial peace had been short lived.

A better deal for women

Women's lives were changing too. By about 1900 many women were working as teachers, journalists and in factories. Some were trying to get into the professions, like law and medicine. The first woman lawyer to graduate and practise in New Zealand was Ethel Benjamin, who was admitted to the Bar in Dunedin in 1897. Other women found that difficulties were put in their way. The first female medical student had human flesh thrown at her in the dissecting room. The one job that was becoming less popular was that of domestic servant. Being a factory worker, typist or telephone operator gave a woman much greater independence and freedom.

Women who worked with their families on farms had always been tough and resourceful. Most farmers depended on their wives to help run the farm. Some women took over the whole management of the farm when their husbands went off to the goldfields or were killed in skirmishes with the Maori.

As far as the law went, women were still very dependent on men. Men owned the property, even if their wives did all the work, and even if their wives had owned the land or property before they had married. Only after 1884 could

Women worked hard on farms.

married women keep their own wages and property. Only men could vote. Men had the advantage in divorce courts and in decisions over custody of the children.

Now women wanted to decide for themselves how they should live. They did not want to be under the authority of a father or a husband. Middle-class women had more free time because they had servants. They had time to lead campaigns for changes in the law.

They wanted better education for girls so that they could become doctors, lawyers, accountants or architects if they wanted to. They wanted to change the laws on marriage, property ownership and divorce. They wanted the right to vote for Members of Parliament and to stand for Parliament themselves. They wanted to use their vote to deal with some of the social problems that affected family life. Such a problem was the 'demon drink'.

The temperance movement

Alcohol was a major problem in New Zealand. It was said that there were only two causes of death — drink and drowning as the result of riding home drunk. The sad case of W. Stoupe, reported in the *New Zealand Herald* in 1886, was not unusual:

Kate Sheppard, organiser of the campaign to give women the right to vote in parliamentary elections.

> A SHOCKING CASE
>
> At the inquest on William Stoupe, grocer, who died suddenly last night, the evidence showed that the deceased had been almost continually drunk for several months. He fell down in a drunken stupor yesterday afternoon, and never awoke. A verdict of death from intoxication was returned.

In the nineteenth century alcoholic drinks were stronger and cheaper than they are today and anyone could buy liquor. Women were distressed by this. Wives were often beaten by drunken husbands. Women (and sometimes children) had to go from pub to pub tracking down their husbands and fathers before they spent all their wages on drink.

In 1885 women formed an organisation to stop the sale of liquor. This was called the Women's Christian Temperance Union. They succeeded in stopping the sale of liquor to children and in doing this they learnt how to organise a campaign. If only women had the vote, they thought, their chance of stopping liquor sales would be so much better. One of the Christchurch leaders, Kate Sheppard,

The members of the first National Council of Women meeting in Christchurch, 1896.

began to organise a campaign for votes for women. This campaign was at its peak from 1890 to 1893. Women wrote articles for newspapers, putting forward the arguments why they should have the vote.

ARE WOMEN CITIZENS?
Yes! *When they are required to pay taxes.*
No! *When they ask to vote.*
DOES THE LAW CONCERN WOMEN?
Yes! *When they are required to obey it.*
No! *When they ask to have a voice in the representation of the country.*

Some politicians like Sir John Hall, Sir George Grey and Sir Robert Stout were sympathetic. Kate Sheppard organised five enormous petitions. The last one, in 1893, was signed by 30,000 adult women — nearly a third of the women in New Zealand.

The strongest opposition came from the drink trade. Men who made their living from making and selling alcohol feared that women would use their vote to have all sales of liquor banned. In spite of opposition from the liquor trade, by 1893 the majority of Members of Parliament were in favour of giving women the right to vote. New Zealand was the first country to do so. By 1919 women were able to stand for Parliament. The first woman Member of Parliament was Elizabeth McCombs, who was elected in 1933.

Children in the 1890s

Campaigning against the 'demon drink' could be fun. A women's temperance band on an outing.

Even though life had become easier for New Zealanders in the 1890s, children were still expected to work hard. Many helped their families run the farm, doing the milking before and after school, and helping with the household chores. If children were sick or someone was hurt in an accident they had to go without medical help or travel miles through the bush to look for a doctor. From an early age they accepted serious responsibilities. A Taupiri family left their fifteen-year-old daughter in charge of the farm for a few days. The nearest doctor was in Hamilton, three-and-a-half hours' ride on a good horse. Later, she described the crisis:

> . . . I was busily doing the washing for twelve folks, when I heard a voice call out, 'Quick, come here; Ella has been eating tutu berries and I think she is dying.' I rushed to the door just in time to see my young sister fall on the ground in convulsions. I picked her up and put her into a bath of hot soap suds. I tried to make her sick by tickling her throat with a long feather, but she became quite unconscious. Then I remembered that when a calf was in that condition, from the same cause, we always bled it by cutting one of its ears. I got a sharp knife and was just going to cut off her right ear, when the thought came to me that perhaps the left ear would be nearer the heart and would bleed more. I turned her over on her right side; she suddenly vomited. I knew that would save her, so her ear was not cut off. A large dose of Epsom salts soon put her right again.

Children helped with farm chores. Here, Lois, Theo and Umi Anthony help their father muster the sheep

Most children were now able to attend primary school. School work was done on slates with a special pencil. Although it squeaked and scratched, a mistake was easy to rub out.

> The uncouth simply spat on the slates and removed the sums with their caps, the more refined breathed on them and used a slate-rag, but the ultra-refined, mainly girls, had a private bottle of water, a rag and a drying-duster.

Lessons were learned by rote, by repeating each point after the teacher in a sing-song fashion. In the towns classes were very large; ninety to a hundred pupils in one class was not uncommon. Discipline was very strict, and the cane and the strap were used often. However, there was a theory that if you held a hair from a horse's tail across your hand, the cane would break in two, or at least lose its power. Another similar theory recommended onion juice to be rubbed in just before the punishment was given.

The annual visit of the school inspector was a very tense occasion. No promotion to the next standard was possible unless the children passed the examination set by the inspector.

Most schools had a horse paddock nearby. After school the children would help each other catch the horses, put sacks on their backs and ride home, two to a horse, in time for milking. Other children had to walk long distances to school. Sometimes they could hop onto the back of a cart or waggon going the same way, but if the driver noticed or if a passerby called out 'Whip behind!', the driver was very likely to use his whip to get them off. In the cities a ha'penny (half a cent) would give them a ride in one of the new electric trams.

These children from Whangape School travelled to school by boat. Some country areas did not have roads.

Below: Geography class, Tararu.

Boys were often in trouble for using shanghais or rifles at the wrong time or in the wrong place. The telephone cups on the new telephone poles were always having to be replaced. In a raid on the little Feilding primary school in 1884 the policeman confiscated thirty catapults. In 1893 there were complaints in Patea that boys were using their guns too close to the main street when they went rabbit shooting. Perhaps it was the hope that special activities would provide an outlet for this energy that led to the founding of youth organisations like the Boys' and Girls' Brigade and the Scouts and Girl Guides.

Most photographs taken of children were very formal. They were often wearing their best clothes, even when they seemed to be doing everyday things.

Home life

At home the kitchen was the centre of family life. With no fast foods and few labour-saving devices, a great deal of time and effort went into preparing and cooking each meal. Some homes would have one of the new kitchen ranges.

Clothes would often be washed by boiling them up in the copper in the shed. Other sheds in the back yard would be for the buggy, a fowl house, even a pigsty. Even people living in towns would have a vegetable garden and a few hens and animals.

Food was cheap, as a Taranaki farmer's daughter described:

> A small loaf of bread was 3d, one pound of butter was 1s, sugar was 2d per lb and was usually bought in 40 lb bags. Flour was about 1d per lb and was bought in 25 lb or 100 lb bags. These bags made very good tea towels.
>
> Eggs were cheap in summer, often 8d per dozen but dear and scarce in winter. A good meal could be had for 1s or 1s 6d and afternoon tea was 6d, with a variety of cakes, scones and sandwiches.
>
> Saturday was the day for shopping and all shops kept open until 10 o'clock; Wednesday was a half holiday.
>
> The baker and butcher called at the door about three times a week to deliver their goods. Meat was cheap; chops about 6d per lb and sausages 2d per lb.

Inside, the house was often papered with old newspapers. Later, proper wallpaper would be pasted over the top. The toilet was usually a small shed at the bottom of the garden, built over a 'long drop'. In the towns sewerage systems usually pumped the sewage out into the harbour at the nearest beach. In some towns it was collected by the 'night cart' and either dumped at the edge of the town or sold to farmers for fertiliser.

Now that life was more settled, New Zealanders began to think about those who could not look after themselves, especially the old and the sick. Organisations like the St John Ambulance Brigade were set up. The Foundation for the Blind, established in 1890, helped blind people learn new trades and reminded the community that the blind had special needs.

'King Dick' Seddon

One group who really needed help were the old people. Many had worked hard all their lives, but because of the long depression they had not been able to save money. They could not work because they were old and weak. Many did not have families to look after them. It fell to the government to help from funds collected from taxation. New Zealand's Prime Minister in the 1890s was Richard John Seddon, known to everyone as 'King Dick'. He was a very popular politician, who had been a miner and pub-keeper from the West Coast and knew how to mix with ordinary people. His speeches were long and wordy but people

Seddon visits London. The winking lion represents the good-humoured reception of the popular New Zealand Prime Minister.

enjoyed his jokes. He had a good memory for names and faces, and cared about people's problems. In 1898 he introduced an old-age pension. It gave old people a small pension (6/11d (nearly 70 cents) per week, raised to 10 shillings ($1) a week in 1905). If they grew a few vegetables, kept a few chickens and spent carefully this was just enough to survive on. Later, in 1911, widows too could get a pension.

Under Seddon's leadership the Liberal Party made some other important changes. Seddon took most of the credit for these improvements, although he had advice and help from public servants like Grace Neill and Edward Tregear. A few free places in secondary schools were introduced for those who had passed an examination at standard six. A system of State fire insurance was begun. Maternity hospitals were set up in the four main centres. They treated poor patients free of charge and trained doctors. They were called St Helen's hospitals after Seddon's birthplace in Lancashire.

New Zealanders admired Seddon's great physical strength and they were charmed by his hearty jokes and good humour. They were proud of his patriotism. But he also represented some of the less likeable characteristics of his time. He wore opponents down by bluster rather than by reasoned argument. By modern standards he was very racist. He opposed Asian immigration into New Zealand and stopped Chinese and Indian settlers from getting the old-age pension. He had been Premier for thirteen years when, in 1906, he died, on his way home from Sydney. Many New Zealanders felt that they had lost a personal friend.

The turn of the century

By 1910 New Zealand had become a more settled place to live in. The telegraph, the rapidly increasing railway network, and the telephone meant that communications were better organised than ever before. When penny postage was introduced on New Year's Day in 1901 it became possible to post letters not just within New Zealand but also to several overseas places for the cost of one penny (one cent). The following year New Zealanders posted thirteen million more letters.

New Zealanders could travel through the country faster and more easily. The North Island Main Trunk Railway was finished in 1908. It had taken forty years to build. Great viaducts and long bridges carried the tracks over steep river gorges. In the South Island a start had been made on the Otira Tunnel through the Southern Alps, which was to link Canterbury and Westland. Settlements, once far from the towns, were isolated no longer. Most of the remote areas had been explored. One of the last was Mount Cook, which was climbed in 1894.

Even sport had become more organised. National organisations, like the New Zealand Rugby Football Union in 1892, were set up to make specific rules for the game. Similarly, cricket, rowing, swimming, tennis, cycling, golf and hockey formed national organisations during the 1880s and 1890s.

Working people became more organised. Trade and professional groups like accountants, architects, journalists, coachmakers, doctors and teachers formed national associations to protect their interests. Trade unions, employers and farmers saw the need to establish nationwide associations. All these organisations showed that people thought of themselves as

A backblocks post office. The introduction of penny postage increased the number of letters posted.

The North Island Main Trunk Railway. The last spike in the line is being driven in by Sir Joseph Ward, the Prime Minister, on 6 November 1908.

A master bakers' conference at Wellington. It was decided to form an association. An executive was established with offices and headquarters in Wellington. They also decided to stop baking hot cross buns on Good Friday – they could just as well be made and delivered on the Thursday before Easter.

part of New Zealand rather than a particular province like Otago or Auckland.

The increased involvement of the government in areas of social welfare, land development, education and health meant that the business of government had to be more highly developed. New government departments administered the new laws throughout the country.

New Zealand was no longer a pioneer land, unexplored and unfamiliar. It was a settled country, prospering in a new era of small farms and country towns. Though many settlers of British origin still felt strong ties with their original homeland, New Zealanders were beginning to develop a sense of being a nation.

TWELVE

The Rise of Farmer Bill

The change from big sheep farms to small family farms was the most important change in New Zealand farming in the early twentieth century. In the nineteenth century farms usually had been either very large — the 'great estates' covering hundreds of hectares — or else quite small holdings where a family grew its own food. Until refrigeration made it possible to sell meat and butter and cheese to people on the other side of the world, there had been no point in trying to grow more food than New Zealanders themselves could eat. There were no big export markets near New Zealand.

Between 1900 and 1920 the family farm of around forty hectares became the most common kind of business in New Zealand. There had been few dairy farms in the 1890s. By 1911 there were more than 15,000. One farm in every three was a dairy farm, and this proportion continued to grow. Other farms produced wool and fat lambs. Most of them did a bit of everything. Nowadays farms are much more specialised than they were in 1910. They choose one product and concentrate on that one. In 1977 an old man, looking around the farming district in Southland where he grew up, scarcely recognised today's farms as the real thing.

When this man, Albert Blanch, was twelve he used to stay on his brother's farm. He loved to help with the working horses. Each one had its own personality.

A team of horses hauling wagons of logs along a track at Te Waewae in Southland. Horses and bullocks were used for all sorts of jobs that were later done by steam engines and tractors.

Children milking cows on a bush farm in 1915.

A six-horse team would stand in the stable munching chaff and oats, each animal a specialist, shafters and leaders. Some preferred to work on either right or left, others liked to be yoked in the middle; there were eager beavers, jibbers and cunning malingerers.

Tractors were not widely used in New Zealand until the 1940s, so at least one good team of horses was a vital part of every farm's equipment, and looking after the horses was a big job. A ploughman's day began about 5.30 a.m. with the horses' first feed. Watering them took twenty buckets of water drawn from the well to fill the yard trough. Harness varied according to the job to be done. It was a 'complicated business of many chains, swingle-trees, spreaders, and the most wonderful thing of all — a single pair of reins from which a full team was controlled along with the spoken word "Giddap"!'

In rough weather the horses were stabled. Bedding them down could take until 10.00 p.m. Six days a week was the regular working week and pay was two to three dollars — plus meals.

There were always cows as well as horses. Dairy farms kept a whole herd, and other farms had one or two cows to provide milk and butter for the family. Milking, separating the cream and making the butter was work for the farmer's wife or daughters. The cows were milked by hand twice each day. In the farm dairy the milk was poured into large earthenware or tin basins to stand for a day. When the cream was 'set' into a thick yellow mass it would be skimmed off into holding jars. The skim milk went to the farm pig and the basins were carefully washed ready for the next day's milk.

About twice a week, out came the wooden churn and in it went the contents of the jars. The cream, either sweet or curdled, went around and around until it turned to butter. Making butter by hand was never easy work. It was always a relief when turned from the churn on to the butter board, where it was salted, carefully weighed and shaped by wooden pats, to be finally wrapped. Some women could produce butter of outstanding flavour, while their sisters could only be satisfied with a good wholesome batch. If the family cows grazed upon wild buttercups or other forbidden fruits they would pass the taint through the milk and into the butter.

Most farms had cats and several kinds of dogs. There were working dogs to herd the animals, a greyhound to hunt rabbits, and also terriers whose special job was rat-catching. At this time the South Island (like much of the North) was infested with rabbits. Boys took their dogs out hunting and sold the rabbit skins. Some boys hunted with ferrets too, but if the ferret killed a rabbit underground he was likely to settle down to sleep off his feast and his owner then had the tiresome job of digging him out.

Life on the land

Work on one of these mixed farms seldom stopped. The whole family was kept busy. Father and sons looked after the fields and animals and crops. Sheep were dipped in the district sheep-dip, providing endless fun for passing boys and dogs. They were shorn with blade shears in the farm shed, and the wool was baled and loaded on to the farm cart to go to the nearest railway station. Pigs were reared and killed to supply home-cured bacon.

Women and older children looked after the farm's vegetable garden and the orchard. Fruit was preserved or made into jam. Women made their own jam jars by beheading beer bottles with a hot iron ring and a bucket of cold water. That trick was a household stand-by until the 1930s. Tasks that usually fell to the children were collecting wood for fires and for the copper in the wash-house, feeding the pig, and finding the eggs hidden around the farm by the free-ranging hens.

Farm life was a richly varied experience. There was lots of hard work but there was also a lot of fun. Usually there was little spare cash in the early days, before the farms were producing well. Children earned their own pocket money. They sold rabbit skins and in the South Island they went bird-nesting. Birds were thought to be pests because they ate grain and seeds. Many county councils paid a bounty of two cents a dozen for birds' eggs and birds' heads. Albert Blanch describes what it was like to collect them:

As I look back upon the art of bird-nesting, I think of the long days spent roaming along the huge gorse fences, some run as wild as a forest where the thrush, blackbird, and the smaller sparrow laid and hatched their eggs. The standard equipment needed was the oldest of clothes, as anything else would soon be in tatters, a stout stick, a treacle tin container, and finally but not least, the ability to remain immune to pain, as prickles, dry or green, turned a lad into a hedgehog. The evenings would be spent in repairs with needle in hand removing any visible thorns, but the concealed prickles embedded in skin announced their presence later on.

Tree-nesting was totally different and this called for some courage and strong nerves. Within walking distance of the township there were some mighty pinus plantations and some giant macrocarpa. Most homes and all farms provided steady work for adventurous lads looking for eggs.

Sparrows shrewdly built their nests on the thinnest branches and highest tops, and much skin was lost in these lofty climbs, but every nest was a challenge. . . The method of collection in the trees was never easy as there were no tins up there. You merely popped the eggs into the mouth and wriggled back to base. Sometimes things went wrong, a sudden jolt causing unpleasant disaster.

When enough eggs and heads were collected they would be taken to the local store for the pay-out.

As starlings and skylarks were regarded as 'goodies', their eggs were not acceptable at the depot. Resourceful boys, however, carefully dotted with ink the pale blue starling eggs and illegally claimed them as thrush eggs. Skylarks produced an egg darker in colour than that of the sparrow although similar in size, so these were cunningly interspersed in the collection and merely became dark sparrow eggs.

At the rear of the stable on a huge manure heap, the eggs and heads would be laid out in rows of one dozen. When this was accomplished, out would come the storekeeper to swiftly count up the bag.

Albert Blanch with his dog 'Sober'. He is wearing a 'Galatea' jacket, moleskin pants and hobnail boots. This photo was taken in 1909.

Farming at this time was a rough and ready business. There was no electricity and not much machinery. There was very little specialisation. It was not until the 1920s that farmers began to make use of scientific knowledge to improve their pasture and animal stocks. The extraordinary success of small farming in the 1900s and 1910s depended on a few basic things: refrigeration, the natural fertility of new soil, cheap land and loans for farmers, and the hard work of the farmers and their wives and children. Small farms replaced big sheep runs in Otago and Southland, and Pakeha families moved on to good land taken or purchased from the Maori after the wars in the North Island. Taranaki, the Waikato and the Bay of Plenty became important dairy-farming districts. Fat lambs were raised in the Wairarapa. Farmers' sons from the South Island came north to break in farms of their own.

The 'drift to the north', which began well before 1900, has continued ever since. The Pakeha population of the North Island passed that of the South Island in 1901. Dunedin had been the most important city in 1880; in 1911 Auckland at 102,676 was clearly the largest. Christchurch was next with 80,193. People were moving north, and they were also moving into towns. Farming was our most important economic activity (probably it still is, because it earns more overseas funds than any other kind of business) but in 1911 the number of people living in towns passed the figure for people living on the land.

New political parties

Changes in New Zealand society were soon followed by political changes. The Liberal Party had been in government for more than twenty years. A whole generation of New Zealanders could not remember a time when the Liberals had not been in power. But by 1911 the party's foundations were crumbling. They had been the party of small farmers and town workers. Farmers whom the Liberals had helped in the 1890s were now doing well. They began to slide away towards a new party led by farmers, the Reform Party. City workers were beginning to support Labour candidates and other radical groups like the 'Red' Federation of Labour, which was formed in 1909. The Liberals were caught. They could not hold both groups of supporters, nor could they cope easily with the drift of population to the north. They had always been strongest in the South Island. Sir Joseph Ward, who took over as Prime Minister when Seddon died in 1906, came from Bluff.

The leader of the Reform Party, 'Farmer Bill' Massey, understood the needs and feelings of farmers. He was one himself. A favourite story about Massey was that in 1894 he had been standing on top of a haystack on his Mangere farm

Prime Minister Bill Massey. This cartoon by the New Zealander David Low was published in the Australian paper the Bulletin.

121

when a telegram was passed up to him on a pitchfork. It was an invitation to stand in a by-election for the west Auckland seat of Waitemata. Massey won that seat and then in the 1896 election he moved to Franklin, which he held until his death on 10 May 1925. In 1911 Massey accused the Liberals of pampering the South Island and neglecting the north. He stumped the North Island asking farmers to vote for the Reform Party.

To farmers a difference existed between lazy 'townies' and hard-working farmers. Once a party was able to present itself as the standard-bearer for the farmers' way of life, the support of country voters was assured.

To everyone's astonishment, the 1911 election was a tie. Including Independents, the Liberals won thirty-eight seats and Reform thirty-eight. There were four Labour members. When Parliament met in February 1912 one MP was overseas, the Speaker was elected, and the parties appeared to be level at thirty-nine seats each, so that the Liberals held on only by the Speaker's casting vote. Ward resigned as Prime Minister and handed the reins to Thomas Mackenzie, but the Liberal Ministry was coming apart at the seams. A change of leader could not save it. At 4.55 on the morning of 6 July 1912 the government lost a confidence vote by forty-one to thirty-three. W. F. Massey, the farmer from Mangere, became Prime Minister on 10 July 1912.

A farmers' government

In Massey's mind New Zealand depended on two things: the hard work and continued prosperity of her farmers, and the British Empire. His Cabinet consisted of wealthy farmers and city businessmen and lawyers. Three of the nine Ministers had been educated at Oxford or Cambridge. Two Ministers, R.H. Rhodes and F.M.B. Fisher, had fought in the Boer War in South Africa. Fisher, who was aged thirty-four, was also a sporting champion. He had represented Canterbury in football and athletics and was three times holder of the New Zealand men's tennis championship. In 1913, when he was a Cabinet minister, he captained the New Zealand tennis team against Great Britain, at Wimbledon.

Massey was not a prime minister who could be expected to sympathise with the difficulties of town workers or the ideas of trade unions. He admired the farming families who worked hard, sent exports to Britain and were 'the backbone of the country'. The town people, by comparison, seemed to him to be parasites living off the wealth the farmers produced. But the towns were growing. More people worked in towns than on farms, and some were envious of the amount of government help the farmers received. And

Houses in Swanson Street, Auckland, being taken down. They were infested by rats and were demolished during a plague scare in 1900.

Epidemic

Disease that affects a lot of people at the same time.

Local authorities

Borough councils, city councils, water boards, etc.

Socialists

People who believe that the community as a whole, rather than individuals, should own most of the means of producing wealth.

there were some real problems at this time. Prices had been rising slowly but since 1900 workers' wages had not always gone up to match them. Standards of living were rising, too. People who could not keep up with the new standards understandably felt very resentful.

Sanitary standards were also changing. Families used to bath once a week in the outside wash-house, heating water in the copper and bailing it into a tin bath on the floor. Now some houses had bathrooms inside with fixed bath tubs and gas water-heaters. Outside toilets with pans collected by the 'night cart' were being replaced by water closets. Rubbish collection had to be arranged with private contractors and paid for. Only the wealthier families had it. Others buried their rubbish or threw it into the backyard or the street. At this time, with the cities growing fast, a clear difference began to emerge in health standards (and smell) between the richer suburbs and the crowded inner-city areas where the workers lived.

People who had to cope with the filth and squalor of the slums also faced a much higher risk of disease. There was fear of plague in Auckland in 1900, and four years later a young man who had been helping to clear dead rats out of a warehouse in Queen Street died of bubonic plague in Auckland Hospital. The Department of Public Health had been set up in 1900 largely to cope with the danger of epidemics spread by the appalling sanitary conditions in our towns. Its main job was to urge local authorities to clean up their water supplies, provide better sewage disposal, and to support vaccination programmes.

Prices of ordinary necessities like rents, food and shoes were rising especially fast. Workers who used to walk to work could now ride bicycles or catch trams, if they could afford to. Working-class families whose men were in steady jobs could hope for greater comfort. But there was a lot of unemployment, especially among unskilled and seasonal workers. It has been estimated that as many as ten percent of workers did not have regular jobs and so were unemployed part of the year. The trade unionists split between a majority who patiently hoped for better times and, on the whole, supported Liberal and Labour candidates for Parliament, and a minority who thought they could get faster results by striking against their bosses.

The 'Red Feds'

The workers who thought they could get better conditions by going on strike were in a few strong unions. They worked at jobs that used large numbers of workers in one place such as the waterfront, railways or mines. Often the work was dangerous and the employers (sometimes overseas companies) were notoriously 'tough'. They tried to keep wages as low as possible and were not inter-

Miners' wives and children walk along the main street of Waihi in a procession in support of the 1912 strike.

ested in safety measures that cost money. In 1909 some of these dissatisfied unions joined the West Coast and Waihi miners to form the Federation of Labour. They were nicknamed the 'Red Feds'. The chief difference between the Red Feds and other unions was that they used the strike as a weapon against their employers. Their leaders, men like the Australian Bob Semple and the New Zealander Pat Hickey, were socialists. The Red Feds were part of a world-wide movement among unskilled workers at that time. They shared many of the ideas of the big American union, the Industrial Workers of the World (IWW, or 'Wobblies'). They read the books written by European and American socialists.

The Red Feds' readiness to strike was new and frightening. All through the Liberal period, strikes were very rare. Between 1894 and 1905 there had been none at all. In 1906 there was only one, and that lasted three hours. After that there were several strikes each year.

In 1912 and 1913 the struggle between the Government and the Red Feds caused the most violent scenes in New Zealand since the wars of the 1860s. At Waihi in May 1912 the miners struck in protest at the engineers' attempt to break away from the main union. There were about a thousand miners at Waihi. Their union was the biggest miners' union in the country. In September the mine owners set up a new union to work the mines. The Massey Government, which took office in July 1912, agreed to protect the new union when the strike-breakers went to work. There were fights between the old and new unionists. More than sixty members of the old union were imprisoned. Many families were driven out of the town. In November a policeman was shot and an engine driver, Fred Evans, was killed. By the time the strike petered out at the end of November the Federation of Labour had been badly damaged. Many of its members left. One lesson

Work and Wages

There is Waihi, with its toil and its
  treasure.
Men's lives are squandered while earning
  a crust.
Leaving homes desolate and a grave for
  some loved one,
Ruthlessly slain by the battery dust.

A Waihi miners' song, collected by Mona Tracey in 1901.

Cossacks

Light cavalry in the Russian army. The Emperors of Russia used the Cossacks to put down riots and rebellions among the Russian peasants and workers.

Scab

A worker who takes the job of a unionist on strike or who refuses to join fellow workers in a protest action or strike.

One of Massey's mounted 'specials' with baton.

of Waihi was that a union could not win a strike against both employers and the Government. Another lesson was that not many New Zealanders agreed with the ideas of the Red Feds. The Waihi miners had fought, and lost, their battle almost alone.

In 1913 the Red Feds tried to reverse the defeat of 1912. When a dispute over shipwrights' travelling allowances in Wellington flared up into a full-scale strike the Government enrolled extra police to keep order. These special policemen, like the ones at Waihi, were mounted and armed with long batons — people called them 'Massey's Cossacks'. Many of them were farmers' sons who were keen to put townies and unions in their place. Others who flocked to join the 'specials' were young clerks and office workers who wanted a bit of excitement and who also welcomed a clash with manual workers. On 30 October excited specials twice rode into crowds in Wellington streets. The strike spread to Auckland, Dunedin and Lyttelton, and in November the army was called out to march through Wellington with fixed bayonets and a machine-gun. W.T. Young, the president of the Federation, told a large crowd that if the employers tried to bring in strike-breakers, as they had done at Waihi, he would 'march on Wellington with 10,000 or 15,000 armed men'. That kind of talk simply hardened Massey's determination to break the strike and the Red Feds with it.

On 8 November a force of over a thousand specials seized control of the Auckland wharves and went on to clear the nearby streets. There was a lot of fighting. At the same time new unions (set up by the employers and known as 'scabs') were starting work on the Wellington and Dunedin wharves. The Federation called for a general strike of all workers to support the wharfies, but very few unions except the miners came to their aid.

The strikers were hopelessly outnumbered and the 1913 strike fizzled out by the end of the year. The last to give in were miners at Huntly, who went back to work in January 1914.

The failed general strike of 1913 seemed to show that the Red Feds were wrong. Tactics that had sometimes succeeded in the big industrial centres of Europe and America did not work in New Zealand, where factories were small and unions weak. But although the leaders of the Federation had been wrong over tactics, they ended up being recognised as people who cared about the needs of New Zealand workers. Paddy Webb, who had been a president of the Federation, was elected to Parliament in

S.C. Smith took this
photograph of mounted
police in Jervois Quay.
Wellington, in 1913.

a by-election in 1913, where he joined the four Labour members, who were sympathetic to the strikers. In by-elections in 1918 Harry Holland, Bob Semple and Peter Fraser were elected. They too had been Red Feds. So were Micky Savage, Tim Armstrong and Bill Parry, who entered Parliament in the general election of 1919. All except Harry Holland (who died in 1933) became ministers in the first Labour Government.

Very few workers had been ready to join the Red Feds in using the strike weapon. But they did not like the tactics that the Government had used to win. The 1914 election was a very bitter contest, especially in the working-class city electorates. When Massey went into Ponsonby he was met by a 'howling mob', who slashed the hood and tyres of his car. Mounted police had to be sent in to rescue him.

From 1908 to 1928 elections were fought by three parties. The Liberals' base was being nibbled away but they continued to win seats, especially in the South Island. Reform's support in the farming community was never absolutely reliable. Even in the cities, where workers were turning towards Labour, a slowly decreasing number of voters still saw the Liberals as their best hope of beating Reform. An election jingle from Auckland in 1914 said:

> Vote, vote, vote for Joey Ward!
> He is sure to win the day.
> For we'll get a salmon tin
> And we'll stick Bill Massey in
> And we'll all shout Hip hip hip hooray!

Prime Minister Bill Massey (left) and Sir Joseph Ward in 1919.

Coalition

Temporary joining of separate parties for a special reason, e.g. to form a government.

It was not so easy. The 1914 election result, as in 1911, seemed a draw. It took six months and several by-elections before the state of the parties was made clear in Parliament. By then Massey had a majority of two. So evenly matched were Liberal and Reform, however, that they formed a loose coalition to run the nation during the First World War, with Massey keeping the prime ministership and Ward taking the deputy's position from 1915 to 1919. Labour stayed out of the wartime government. It eventually benefited from the growing disillusionment as the war dragged to a close at the end of 1918.

A changing society

The changes in New Zealand life in the early years of the twentieth century can be summed up as follows: the shift to small farming; the movement north; the growth of towns; the end of the Liberals' political dominance. There was one more important change. Families were getting smaller. Women who married in 1880 had had, on average, six or seven children. The average number of children born to women who married in the early 1920s was two or three. The move to smaller families happened between the 1890s and the First World War. It began in the towns. Country families remained quite large until the 1930s and 1940s: there was so much to

do on farms that a big family was a useful asset. In the towns smaller families lived in smaller households. Organisations were set up to look after old people and sick people. There were fewer servants. An ordinary household in the 1920s consisted of a man and his wife and their two or three children.

District nurses with their bicycles outside the South Durham Street Nursing Headquarters in Christchurch in 1914.

Most women at this time worked for some years between school and marriage. Few women worked outside their homes after marriage. Inside their homes they probably worked as hard as ever. It became fashionable to look at motherhood and home-making as women's only true career; if they wanted to use their brains they should do so by running their houses on scientific principles. In 1909 the University of Otago began teaching home science and three years later the subject was made a separate university degree.

In 1907 Dr Frederick Truby King and his wife formed the Plunket Society. Its proper name was the Royal New Zealand Society for the Health of Women and Children, but it was called Plunket after its first patron, Lord Plunket, the Governor-General. Plunket's purpose was to train mothers to rear healthy babies. At this time fifty-one out of every thousand babies died in the first year, usually from diarrhoea and sicknesses caught from bad feeding and poor hygiene. Although this figure was only half as high as the death rate for babies in Britain, it was very worrying to a new country with a small population. Plunket nurses stressed the importance of cleanliness and absolutely regular feeding timetables. Babies' health and growth were carefully checked. District nurses did the same work in country areas. The Health Department carried out regular health checks in schools after 1912. The idea that children were valuable to New Zealand and that society was responsible for helping parents to look after them began to be widely accepted at about this time.

The long process of change from a nineteenth-century settler society to a recognisably modern New Zealand took twenty years or more. It began in the 1890s and went on through the 1920s. The process was at first interrupted and then greatly accelerated by the First World War, which broke out in August 1914.

THIRTEEN

The Maori People Rebuild

Maori workers penning sheep on a rugged farm in the Bay of Plenty in 1922.

Very few Maori lived in towns at the end of the nineteenth century. They lived in their own villages. Most of the best land had been sold or had been taken from them by the Government during the wars of the 1860s. Tribes who still held good farming land often felt that it was useless to try to hold on to it now that the Pakeha were so clearly in control, and so they sold what they had left. Much of the remaining Maori land was hard to farm or so far away from roads and towns that the settlers did not want it. The Tuhoe people, for example, lost the fertile flat lands of the Bay of Plenty and moved back into the harsh hill country of the Ureweras. The Waikato tribes had half a million hectares of their fertile river lands taken from them and were forced into the 'King Country' — the lands of the Ngati Maniapoto tribe, who supported them.

It was very hard to earn money once the land was gone. Some Maori worked for Pakeha farmers, others dug for kauri gum or gathered flax. South Island Maori collected mutton birds. Tribes who lived near the bush or the sea caught the food they had always eaten — pigeons, eels and fish.

Houses were built in the old ways — of nikau, ponga, raupo, bark and earth.

In the South Island sod walls were used because they were warmer. Sleeping houses were small and crowded. Usually there were no toilets. It was hard to keep the outdoor kitchen areas clean. Water for drinking and washing had to be collected from the nearest stream.

Life was not always uncomfortable in these houses. Eruera Stirling went to live with his grandparents in a whare in the bush when he was a small child.

> Our toetoe hut was pretty nice. It was warm and well kept, made out of nikau and ponga and toetoe, with plaited mats, a special place to light the fire, and a window and two holes at the top to let out the smoke. . . At night after the fire was kindled I lay on my sleeping-mat and Pera and Hiria lay on theirs, and I watched the smoke lift and rise through the air to the outside.
>
> I enjoyed staying with the old people because I got plenty to eat, they gave me the best of food. We ate berries — taraire, tawa, karaka and miro cooked in the hangi; pigeons, tui and parrots cooked in their own fat and kept in calabashes; wild pigs and fish, but one of the special delicacies my grandparents liked was the kiore, the grey rat — that was their special.

A little girl cuddles her pet piglet outside her home in a Maori kainga in Northland.

A separate society

Most Maori families lived quite apart from the Pakeha society that was growing up around them on the land they used to own. Sometimes a tribe would meet together at a hui or a tangi. These gatherings might draw several thousand people. When Tawhiao, the Maori King, died in 1894 his tangi lasted more than a month and 4,000 people followed his body to Taupiri mountain where he was buried. Usually, though, Maori settlements were small, with fewer than fifty people, and life in the villages was extremely hard.

The most frightening problem was sickness. Maori had no natural resistance to Pakeha diseases. Their poor housing helped diseases like tuberculosis and typhoid to spread extraordinarily fast. Many had died in the wars, many more died of sicknesses that rarely killed the Pakeha, like measles, whooping cough and flu.

When Captain Cook visited New Zealand in 1769 the Maori population was probably more than 100,000. By 1896 their numbers had fallen to 42,113. That was the lowest number recorded. By 1901 their numbers had begun to rise; there were then 45,500 Maori, ninety-five percent of them living in the country.

Maori did not always think of themselves as the 'Maori people'. They still regarded themselves as members of tribes. Their ways of living were based on the

Tents set up as a hospital for victims of a typhoid epidemic at Maungapohatu in January 1925. This outbreak of disease affected children very badly. Two children died.

Te Rangi Hiroa graduating in medicine from the University of Otago.

tribe and they looked to their own people in their own areas for leadership. Though many Maori had lost their land and were struggling to survive not all tribes were affected equally. Some, like the Ngati Porou of the East Coast, had not had land taken from them. They were fairly well off and competed quite successfully with the Pakeha.

The first Maori to gain a university degree was Apirana Ngata of Ngati Porou, who finished a BA at Canterbury in 1893 and then moved to Auckland where he finished a law degree in 1896. In 1905 he went into Parliament as Member of Parliament for Eastern Maori.

The Young Maori Party

Ngata was born at Te Araroa in 1874. When he was ten years old he was sent to Te Aute College in Hawke's Bay. In the 1880s and 1890s Te Aute produced a group of young men who were determined to use their education to help their people. They called themselves the Young Maori Party. Ngata was one of them; Peter Buck (Te Rangi Hiroa) from Taranaki was another. He went to Otago and studied medicine and was a Native Health Officer from 1905 to 1909. He became MP for Northern Maori in 1909, was briefly a minister in Mackenzie's Government, and then he went away to the First World War. In 1927 Buck left New Zealand to become director of the Bishop Museum in Hawaii. Later he was a professor at Yale University in America. Maui Pomare was at Te Aute from 1889 to 1892. Like Te Rangi Hiroa, he

became a doctor and was a Native Health Officer from 1901 to 1911 when he became MP for Western Maori. He was a minister in the Reform Government from 1912 to 1928 and for three of those years was minister of Health.

Sir Apirana Ngata as an old man leading a haka at New Zealand's Centennial Celebrations at Waitangi in 1940.

The Young Maori Party believed that Maori must adopt some of the Pakeha ways of life. They urged them to copy Pakeha health care and to succeed in the Pakeha education system, as they themselves had done. Ngata had some success, especially with the Ngati Porou, in untangling complicated Maori land rights, so that Maori owners could more easily gather together scattered pieces of land and set up profitable sheep and dairy farms.

Young Maori Party leaders like Buck and Pomare, and Frederick Bennett of Te Arawa, who became an Anglican bishop, achieved success in the Pakeha world. Some others were able to follow their example. But for most Maori in the 1890s and the early twentieth century, competition was not the answer. Maori customs stressed co-operation and helping one another. In Pakeha society success for one person was often achieved at the cost of failure for others. That was not the Maori way. Also, competition with the Pakeha was simply impossible for most Maori at this time. They had lost too much. Land was the basis of success in New Zealand and the best land had been taken or sold. Government help was poured out to Pakeha farmers by the Liberal and Reform Governments. There was plenty of cheap loan money to develop Pakeha farms. There was none for Maori farmers.

Schools and hospitals were now built for Pakeha. Maori parents could not pay for books and there was usually nowhere in a Maori house for children to do homework. People who went to hospital had to pay, and Maori could not pay. Even if they could they were often unwelcome, being believed to carry diseases. In 1906 only four doctors in the Waikato area would take Maori patients. The gap between Maori and Pakeha was simply too wide for most Maori to jump. They had to build up their own society again before they could survive in the wider New Zealand society.

When the rebuilding began, it happened within the separate tribes: different leaders appeared at different times and places. Sometimes a leader would encourage a large tribe or group of tribes; often leadership was on a smaller scale — one important family helping others in their district. Leadership networks were sometimes made stronger by the custom of taumau (arranged marriages). Eruera Stirling's parents, Mihi Kotukutuku and Duncan Stirling, had their marriage arranged for them. When Eruera was at Te Aute he was called home to be married. This is how he described what happened:

> My mother was very pleased to see me and she said, 'Well, Eruera, you are going to be married very soon.'
>
> I said to my mother, 'No, Mum, I don't want to get married yet!'
>
> 'Now boy, you listen to me. We have already arranged a wife for you, and she's coming here today, too! You have to marry this woman, because if you don't I'll have to pay very heavily for it.'
>
> She explained to me that if I cut back the taumau promise, she would have to give those people a lot of land to pay for it, and she didn't want to do that. I tried to say something but it was no use. . .

Amiria O'Hara, the girl chosen to marry him, was not happy about the arrangement either. She tried to run away. But in the end Eruera and Amiria did marry and had a long and happy life together, living until the 1980s.

Another type of arranged marriage took place when a leader needed a helper.

When Princess Te Puea of Waikato was thirty-eight years old her family chose a much younger man to marry her so that he could be her companion and helper. He was called Tumokai — the worker.

Maori leadership

The task of rebuilding Maori society was extraordinarily difficult. It could be done only by leaders whom the people trusted. They trusted their own leaders and were not willing to listen to outsiders. The most effective leaders belonged to their people, not only because they were Maori but because they were from the same tribe or group of tribes. Although the leaders and the methods were different in different tribes, the general pattern was much the same: first the people had to trust the leader and be prepared to follow his or her advice, then some way of earning money had to be found so that housing, health care and education could be organised. As life improved, the spirit and confidence of the people started to grow again.

Some of the new leaders started Maori religions. The importance of these religions was that they were able to explain the world to Maori in ways that made sense to them. Also they linked the present harsh realities of life to a hopeful future. If the people trusted in their religion and their prophets, God would help them. Rebuilding was never an easy task. It was encouraging to feel that God and the wairua (the spirits of their ancestors) were on their side. One such religion was Ringatu, which was founded by Te Kooti Rikirangi. Many of Te Kooti's teachings reminded his people of the story of the Jews in the Old Testament, who had been driven out of the land of Israel and wandered in the wilderness until God brought them back to Jerusalem. The Maori, too, had lost their land and been harshly treated by men in power. Te Kooti taught his people to beware of the Pakeha. A Ringatu waiata (song) says:

> *The devious cleverness of the white man*
> *Has been inspired by whom?*
> *Why, by Satan of course.*
> *Therefore beware of the temptations,*
> *the pitfalls of the Pakeha*
> *And don yourselves with the strength to resist.*

Te Kooti taught them that in his matakite (visions) he had been promised that God would save the Maori just as He had saved the Jews. This gave them hope and confidence for the future. As late as 1981 the Ringatu religion was followed by 6,114 Maori, mostly in the Bay of Plenty and the East Cape. One of these later Ringatu wrote:

To believe in Te Kooti is to believe that one day Maori grievances will be no more, that our salvation is surely near at hand. Without this I can only see a depressing future, as the Pakeha does not look as if he is going to give up the reins yet.

Rua's new Jerusalem

Rua Kenana.

Below: Children playing on a mud slide outside the school at Maungapohatu about 1921.

As Te Kooti lay dying he said, 'In twice seven years a man shall arise in the mountains to succeed me. He shall be the new prophet of the people.' Rua Kenana said that he was that man. He called himself Te Mihaia Hou, the new Messiah. As Te Kooti had done, Rua used the sufferings of the Jews to explain the present suffering of the Tuhoe people. His followers called themselves Nga Iharaira (the Israelites), and his settlement at Maungapohatu, in the Urewera hills, was called New Jerusalem. Rua promised the Tuhoe that their lands would be returned and that Pakeha rule would come to an end. At its peak, Rua's New Jerusalem attracted over a thousand people, mostly from the Tuhoe and Whakatohea tribes. Maungapohatu was very isolated and few Pakeha had ever been there. Strange stories were told by people who knew nothing about Rua and who were afraid of Maori prophets.

During the First World War Pakeha fears began to centre upon Rua's attitude to the war. He told his followers that the time for fighting was past. They should not fight in the Pakeha war. It was a short step from that to the Pakeha believing that Rua was on Germany's side. People began to call Rua 'the Maori Kaiser' and to talk about the New Jerusalem as Rua's 'stronghold'. The government decided to arrest him.

In March 1916 the invasion of Maungapohatu was planned. Seventy police were sent in three groups. There were a large number of mounted police, some of whom had been at Waihi in 1912. Because Rua's village was so remote, the police had to take a lot of gear and camp on the way. They

The wooden circular temple at Maungapohatu was built in 1906, and demolished in 1916.

moved like a small army with waggons and pack-horses. They were convinced that when they reached Maungapohatu there would be a fight. In fact there was no resistance. Rua came to meet them with his two eldest sons, Whatu and Toko. But when the police moved suddenly to seize Rua there was a scuffle and a gun went off. No one knows whose. Immediately there was panic. The police had been expecting an ambush and thought this was it. Toko Rua ran for his gun and wounded four policemen before he was shot and killed. Toko's best friend, Te Maipi, was also killed. Rua, Whatu and four others were arrested.

Rua was charged with sedition (a kind of treason). His trial in the Auckland High Court lasted forty-seven days. It was the longest trial in New Zealand history until 1977. None of the charges against Rua based on the events of 2 April could be made to stick, but he was found guilty of a lesser offence — being unwilling to be arrested at Te Waiiti on 12 February. The judge sentenced him to twelve months' hard labour and eighteen months' imprisonment, a very heavy sentence. Eight members of the jury signed a petition protesting at the harsh treatment of Rua.

The cost of defending themselves at the trials that followed the raid on Maungapohatu, and the cost of the raid itself, which the Maori had to pay, almost ruined Rua's people. They had to sell much of their land and all their animals. Pleas for help were met with indifference. 'No anxiety need be felt as to Rua's wives or children starving. Natives always help one another and if ever they become short of food they will either go back to their own people, or get married to other Natives,' reported an official sent to look into their desperate plight.

When Rua returned to his followers in 1918 he found them much poorer. Many people had left the settlement, but others stayed with him until his death on 20 February 1937. Some still believe that he will return to them, as he promised.

The Ratana religion

Tahupotiki Wiremu Ratana was also a religious leader. He was not well educated like the leaders of the Young Maori Party, nor was he from among the chiefs. He was a farmer who lived near Wanganui. As a young man he had led a fairly wild life, and then on 8 November 1918 he saw a vision. A voice from a cloud spoke to him and told him to 'unite the Maori people'. All through the summer of 1918–19 the news of Ratana's vision spread. A stream of people came to his farm. Many of them brought sick relatives and Ratana healed them. Three thousand gathered to hear him speak on Christmas Day 1920. Four marquees and 130 tents were needed to shelter them. The place later became Ratana Pa.

Some of Ratana's followers were his own people, the Ngati Apa and Ngati Raukawa. But people also came from all over New Zealand, from many different tribes. Ratana himself travelled up and down the country speaking to all Maori. He brought special encouragement to Maori who had moved to cities and towns and were losing touch with their tribal leaders. In May 1925 he announced the formation of the Ratana Church. In 1928 he decided that four of his followers should stand for Parliament. He could see that government money was spent to help Pakeha New Zealanders and he wanted a strong voice for ordinary Maori in Parliament.

The first Ratana Member of Parliament was Eruera Tirikatene, who won Southern Maori in a by-election in 1932. When Labour won the 1935 election Ratana went to see the Prime Minister, 'Micky' Savage, at Parliament Buildings. He placed on the table a potato, a broken gold watch, a greenstone tiki, and a huia feather. Savage looked at these things and asked Ratana to explain what they meant. The potato was the ordinary Maori who needed his land because 'a potato cannot grow without soil'. The watch was broken, like the law which protected Maori land; the law of the new government must repair the

Tahupotiki Wiremu Ratana.

Ratana arriving at Taupo in the 1920s. He is holding a Ratana flag. Many of the Maori leaders designed their own flags and banners, which their followers still treasure.

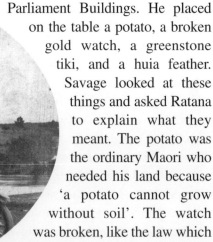

138

broken law of the old one. The tiki stood for the spirit of the Maori. If Savage protected the Maori people he would earn the right to wear the huia feather, which was the sign of a chief. After Ratana's visit to Savage most Maori supported the Labour Party, and all four Maori seats were held by Labour from 1943 until 1993. The votes of Maori members twice kept Labour Governments in power, 1946–49 and 1957–60.

Ratana died on 18 September 1939. His message to his people was that they could survive in a Pakeha world — even in the cities. The angels would strengthen those who believed. The Ratana religion gave them confidence and Ratana's practical advice helped them to manage in the modern world.

Princess Te Puea

Princess Te Puea Herangi, of Waikato, was a different kind of leader. She was born to the task of leadership. Her mother was the eldest child of King Tawhiao. She died in 1898 when Te Puea was fifteen and from that time Te Puea was recognised as one of the leaders of her mother's people. The Waikato tribes were extremely bitter about the losses they had suffered during the wars. They did not want anything to do with Pakeha ways, especially Pakeha doctors and Pakeha schools where Maori children had to speak English. Te Puea herself had had three years at school, but this was unusual. In 1905 there were probably 2,000 Waikato children who had no schools.

Princess Te Puea Herangi.

The tribe was also very poor. The King's village near Mercer was on low ground, which sometimes flooded in winter. It had no meeting house. In 1913 there was a terrible smallpox epidemic. Many people died. Te Puea said: 'I found that Maori people were dying by the riverside. We could get no nurses for them. I had very little money so all my sister and I could do was to make a camp from nikau palms . . . [and] we nursed as many as possible. . .' In 1918 there was another epidemic — the 'Spanish flu'. Te Puea's husband remembered that only three out of the 200 people in the village did not get sick. Fifty died in that village alone. No one knew what to do as the epidemic raged all through the Waikato. There was no help from outside. No one in the world knew how to cope with the new virus at that time. Te Puea's husband, Tumokai, said:

> Nobody knew what they should be doing. One person told us not to drink water and we believed it for a while. Then one of the ones who was ill went mad and jumped into the river and drank water frantically. He got better. Others, my sister among them, were crying out for water, their mouths all burnt. And we didn't give them any. And they died. We just didn't know what we should have done.

After disasters like these Te Puea decided to move the King's village to a place near where the first Maori King's house had been at Ngaruawahia. It was to be called Turangawaewae (a place to stand). There she would help them to build a new home where they would be able to live healthier lives free from the constant threat of early death. She said to them, 'We may find it easier to die here than to live there. But we have to go. And we are going to build a marae there that will be suitable for everybody throughout the country; a marae that, one day, people will visit from all over the world. And we're going to do it for Waikato and for our king.' Turangawaewae was to be a sign that Waikato could rebuild; and if Waikato could do it, then so could other tribes.

Building Turangawaewae was such an enormous task that it attracted the attention of Maori, and also many Pakeha, from all over New Zealand. In 1928 Gordon Coates, the Prime Minister, visited Te Puea there, and when the meeting house Mahinarangi was opened in 1929 the celebration hui drew 6,000 Maori from many tribes. Ngata brought a thousand visitors from the East Coast.

Te Puea showed that Maori were able to help themselves. She taught the importance of Maori values and showed how much could be done when people helped one another. She taught them to remember Maori culture — songs, stories, dances, and tribal histories. She took care that the arts of carving and canoe building were not lost. Above all, Te Puea stressed the value and importance of children. After the 1918 epidemic she travelled through the Waikato and brought more than a hundred orphans back with her. All her life she collected children around her and found time to talk to them and teach them.

Te Puea also taught her people that some Pakeha ways of doing things could be useful to them. Turangawaewae had a proper sewerage system and a clean water supply. She persuaded the Waikato to send their children to school. When they were sick she encouraged them to go to doctors. In 1943 the meeting house Mahinarangi was turned into a medical clinic with a visiting doctor and Maori came from as far away as Tuakau and Te Kuiti to see their 'own' doctor.

Maori society revives

The work Te Puea was doing built Maori confidence in themselves as Maori so that they could then reach out and make use of Pakeha things as well. There were other leaders like her doing the same work in other tribes: Whina Cooper of Te Rarawa, Hone Heke Rankin of Ngapuhi, Taiporoutu Mitchell of Te Arawa, and Hoeroa Marumaru of Rangitikei were such people.

The worst time for Maori society seems to have been the end of the nineteenth century. That was when their numbers were fewest. The twentieth century has seen a dramatic recovery. As Maori adjusted to European diseases and as knowledge of proper sanitation spread the death rate dropped. In 1936 there were 82,000 Maori and by 1951 there were 115,676. In 1991, those who identified themselves in the census as Maori numbered 434,847 (12.9 % of the population).

In the 1920s and 1930s governments began to pay more attention to Maori

A district nurse checking
the health of Maori
children in Northland.

needs. In earlier times it seemed as though they had taken notice of Maori only when they wanted Maori land. Now they began to help. In the 1930s money began to be spent on housing. More Maori children started to go to high school. Eight Maori district high schools were set up in the 1940s. Money was lent to Maori farmers for land development. Some of the land that had been unfairly taken during the wars was returned.

In the early days some Maori were famous in their tribes for their oratory or skill as warriors. The mana of a great chief sometimes made him famous among many tribes. In this century some Maori have become heroes for all New Zealanders. Maori sportsmen are clear examples of this. Maori played in the first rugby team New Zealand sent overseas. It went to New South Wales in 1884 and won all of the eight games. All Blacks like George Nepia, Sid and Ken Going, Mac Herewini, Tane Norton, 'Tiny' Hill, Buck Shelford and Frank Bunce were all heroes in their time. William Pember Reeves saw Nepia play at fullback against England in 1925 and wrote a poem about him:

> *Kia toa! New Zealand see*
> *Nepia guards the gate*
> *A rock and house of defence is he*
> *A tino-tangata great.*

Maori entertainers like Howard Morrison and opera singers Inia Te Wiata (who died in 1971) and Kiri Te Kanawa have fans all over the world.

In the 1940s a major new change in Maori life took place. Maori began to move into the towns. The amount of land they had left was not enough to support their growing numbers. City life was also interesting. Whereas in 1890 ninety-five percent of Maori lived outside towns, in 1990 most lived in towns and cities.

George Nepia kicks for touch, 1928.

More changes were needed. The move to the cities sometimes unravelled ties between family and tribe. A new sense of being Maori began to grow alongside the idea of belonging to a particular tribe. New city marae were built by Maori from many tribes. The Maori Women's Welfare League was set up in 1951, and the New Zealand Maori Council in 1962. These were for all Maori, not for particular tribes.

Living in cities has often been difficult for Maori families. They are larger than Pakeha families and usually poorer. But city life has also provided excitement and new opportunities. Maori have come together in greater numbers than they were able to do before. The Maori population of Auckland, for example, was over 69,000 in 1984. Many more Maori are going to secondary schools, to technical institutes and to universities.

New groups and new leaders have appeared. Some younger Maori have formed gangs. Some groups protest at Maori grievances. In 1975 Whina Cooper formed Te Roopu O Te Matakite (The People with a Vision) and led a march from the far north to Wellington to protest against the taking of Maori land. Concerns about the survival of the Maori language led to initiatives such as the Kohanga Reo (language nests) for pre-schoolers. Many Maori felt that they had been shortchanged by the Pakeha over land, fishing rights, language and customs. In an attempt to investigate, a special tribunal was set up in 1975 to hear the gievances and to advise the government what should be done. The powers of this Waitangi Tribunal have been extended and

Wayne 'Buck' Shelford

many claims have been registered with it. Some, such as that of the Ngati Whatua about the return of Bastion Point, were upheld by the tribunal and accepted by the government. Many other claims are still to be settled. In politics too, new parties developed. In 1979 Matiu Rata, Ranginui Walker, Pat Hohepa and others formed Mana Motuhake (The Separate Mana of the People). In its first general election it gained the support of about 15 percent of Maori voters. After the first MMP election in 1996, the New Zealand First Party represented Maori aspirations in Parliament.

Frank Bunce

There are many Maori voices to be heard. They speak for Maori as well as, or instead of, separate tribes. They also speak up for Maori language and culture. Te Puea's dream that these things should be taught to all New Zealand children, and not just to Maori children, is slowly coming to pass. There are some Maori radio and television programmes and Maori studies is taught in most schools, technical institutes and universities. Pakeha children are learning how to behave correctly on a marae.

The Maori people have come nearer to Pakeha society in the last eighty years, and they have brought valuable Maori traditions with them to share with all New Zealanders.

Whina Cooper speaking to the first meeting of the Maori Women's Welfare League in 1951.

Waitangi Tribunal members John Turei, John Clarke and Areta Koopu with other tribunal members and local Maori during the hearings on the Tauranga claim, August 1997.

Above: The Minister for Treaty Settlements, the Hon. Doug Graham, meets Hinerau Te Kani at Opotiki Marae.

Left: Not all Maori have been satisfied with the settlements offered. When the government announced that there would be a limit on the amount of compensation available, this modern Maori warrior trampled the so-called 'fiscal envelope' underfoot.

A major factor in the success of the Ngaki Tamariki programme has been the enthusiastic involvement of sports stars like former Manu Samoa captain Peter Fatialofa.

Above: Children can now attend Kura Kaupapa. Maori language immersion schools.

Left: Te Wharekura pupils Stephanie Martin and Kaawariki Morgan outside their purpose-built school.

FOURTEEN

The Growth of a Nation

In the nineteenth century New Zealand and the six Australian colonies, such as New South Wales and Victoria, were known as 'Australasia'. All seven were British colonies. Their peoples were mainly British. They spoke English. It was often thought that one day these colonies might all join together as one country. In the 1890s the Australian colonies decided to form a federation, with a central government, but leaving the colonial governments (which became the present-day state governments) with some powers.

Some New Zealanders, especially some farmers who exported food to Australia, wanted this country to throw in her lot with Australia, and become a state within the federation. But most New Zealanders did not want to do that. One leading politician, Sir John Hall, said that the 1,100 miles of the Tasman Sea were 1,100 arguments against joining. When the Australians established their Commonwealth in 1901, New Zealand stayed aloof.

The Prime Minister, Richard Seddon, was opposed to New Zealand joining Australia. He thought that New Zealand could not only become 'the Britain of the South', but should get its own empire. He wanted New Zealand to take over Fiji, Samoa and other Pacific Islands so that it would be the centre of another 'federation', big enough to compete with Australia. Julius Vogel and Sir George Grey had had the same ambition. To many people the idea of such a small colony aiming to become an imperial power was ridiculous. The poet Allen Curnow later wrote of Vogel and Seddon

> *howling empire from an empty coast,*
> *A vast ocean laughter*
> *Echoed unheard . . .*

New Zealand was later to get some small islands, including the Cook Islands and, after the First World War, Western Samoa. But no 'empire'.

It is doubtful whether many people really wanted an empire, but probably most people in New Zealand thought that eventually the New Zealanders would form a nation of their own. They knew that the Americans — and now the Australians — had become new nations. They thought that New Zealand should do so too. In 1890 one man said, 'We are here the pioneers of a great nation.'

By 1886 more than half of the Pakeha living in New Zealand had been born here. They had no memories of the British 'Motherland'. The land they loved was the one in which they grew up. But most of them had no say in the government of the country — they were children, and too young to vote. Of the European population of 578,500, some 300,000 had been born in New Zealand. But, of these, only 43,500 were aged over twenty; 215,000 were under fifteen and 256,000 were under twenty-one. That meant that the grown-ups who ran the country — the government, the farms, the businesses, the schools and so on — had mostly been born in Great Britain. Most of them still thought of themselves as British. Sir Harry Atkinson, Premier 1887–90, said that:

> It has been said by some honourable gentlemen that they are proud of New Zealand: and so am I. They say they hope New Zealand is going to rise to be a great nation. I have no such hope; but I hope and believe that we are going to be an important part of a great nation. . . . I am proud of being an Englishman as well as a New-Zealander — but, if I had to choose between the two, I should choose to be an Englishman rather than a New-Zealander.

People with such opinions wanted New Zealand to stay a British colony, a child in the arms of the motherland, and not grow up to be independent.

The growth of a nation

There were some changes occurring in New Zealand that were encouraging the growth of national unity and feeling. In the early days the settlements were almost completely cut off from one another except by sea. People spoke of 'the six colonies of New Zealand'. A person would say, 'I'm an Aucklander', or 'I'm a Wellingtonian', not 'I'm a New Zealander'.

The construction of roads and railways in the later nineteenth century broke down the isolation of the settlements. So did the construction of telegraphs and the spread of post offices. In 1860 it could take weeks for a letter from Auckland to reach, say, Dunedin. Now this was changing. In 1882 New Zealanders sent 1,500,000 telegrams. Equally important was the installation of telephones: there were 5,000 by 1896, 12,000 by 1904. It was now possible to have national organisations because people could keep in touch. Previously, sport, for instance, was a purely provincial activity. Now in 1892, as we have seen, the New Zealand Rugby Football Union was established; in 1896 the National Council of Women was founded; in 1889 the New Zealand Brass Bands Association. Very many more national organisations date from that time.

The Boer War

The first clear signs that many New Zealanders were beginning to feel that they were a new people are to be found during the Boer War, from 1899 to 1902. That was a war in which the British Army, helped by the Australians, Canadians and

Boys of the Southern Cross

We've heard about your trouble, Tom,
In rousting out the Boer;
You shall not fight out there alone
Amid the cannon's roar,
The blood that stirr'd our noble sires
To build up England's Fame,
Re-kindles in Colonial sons
Their prestige to maintain. For —

We are boys of the Southern Cross,
Our stars shine on our flags —
Emblazoned with the Union Jack,
To show we're Empire lads.

With three cheers for the Empire, loud;
And for the Queen, — Hurray!
We'll stick tight in our saddles, boys,
To drive the foe away;
When once again our land shall loom
And Kruger is no more,
Welcome we our native home —
And fair New Zealand's shore.

A patriotic poem written when New Zealand troops went to the Boer War.

New Zealanders, conquered two small Boer countries in southern Africa. Most New Zealanders became wildly excited about winning the war and did not ask whether it was just. Many of the Boers were guerrillas — they fought the British for a while and then went home to their farms. The British retaliated by burning the farmhouses, looting the animals and putting the women and children in 'concentration camps'. Thousands of them died of diseases. Of course the public did not know this for some time.

New Zealand was the first colony to send troops, a contingent of mounted infantry. There was great excitement. When they sailed from Wellington in October 1899 the biggest crowd ever gathered in New Zealand, about 50,000 people, turned out to give them a good send-off. When the troops marched to the wharf, a newspaper reported, 'grizzly-bearded veterans' strode alongside them. The children were as excited as the grown-ups. 'Bare-footed little toddlers . . . strove so wearily to keep pace with the men.' They 'wanted the "big sojers" to share their sweets with them'.

When the second contingent left in January 1900 many of the adults were sad, but not the children's choir.

From their high position on the singing stand they contemplated their surroundings, and were content to wave their flags and chatter and laugh, not thinking of the serious element of the demonstration, and enjoyed the passing scene, with all its life and movement. For them the march past, the bright and varied uniforms of the soldiery, the flutter of the flags, the glitter of the bayonets, the galloping of the escorts, and the manoeuvring of the yachts and boats on the glass-like waters of the harbour, combined with the sense of their own importance, was a present enjoyment which overmastered every other consideration.

They were the first to see the marching men: first the medalled veterans, and then the volunteers, in their coloured uniforms. And it was their hurrahs which swelled the one great shouting chorus of the day when the contingent came marching into line and swung into column formation in readiness for the speech-making ordeal. Over the heads of the choir, in the national colours, were the words, 'The children of New Zealand wish you God-speed and a safe return'.

148

The First Contingent
marching from Karori,
Wellington, towards the
wharves to sail to the
South African war,
October 1899. You can see
the children watching.

Girls at a Dunedin floral fete in 1900, raising funds to send the Rough Riders off to war. The girls in the parade wore fancy aprons and caps and carried flowers. Cartons of sweets and cakes were sold in decorated stalls. They also sold enamel brooches bearing pictures of the British generals. There was an afternoon tea tent. The little girl second from the left was 'Phyl' Ward. Her group won the first prize in their section. They wore dresses covered with white daisies sewn on overnight for freshness, and the borders and hoops were decorated with yellow daisies. Phyllis Ward says she was annoyed with the girl on her right for wearing a bonnet when they were supposed to wear green caps. Her father took the photograph.

Trooper Ireland of the Third Contingent escapes from the Boers under heavy fire. This is the war as an artist imagined it when drawing an illustration in a magazine. It was titled 'Plucky Deed by New Zealanders'.

School children raised money for the Patriotic Fund. Those in Otago and Southland raised £500 ($1,000) in a few months.

When they reached South Africa the New Zealanders quickly made a name for themselves. Most of them were New Zealand born and on average they were much bigger than the British soldiers. They proved excellent scouts, for they were used to galloping in open country, sleeping out and roughing it. The newspapers began to claim that the 'Maorilanders' (as they were sometimes called) were about the best soldiers in South Africa. Some of the soldiers boasted in their letters home about how good they were. Sergeant Gourlay from Dunedin, who was killed shortly afterwards, wrote to his brother that the 'regular' British soldiers were 'not up to much as riders. We can beat them bad, and the authorities reckon us the very best at reconnoitring and patrolling.'

The New Zealand 'Rough Riders', as those in several contingents were called, certainly proved that they were as bold and brave as the best of the British or other colonial troops or the Boers. In one of the first actions in which the New Zealanders took part, some seventy men, led by Captain Madocks, charged a party of a hundred Boers who had attacked some soldiers from Yorkshire. Two New Zealanders were killed but they drove the Boers right back. The 'Yorks' stood and cheered. The hill was named 'New Zealand Hill'.

A sense of pride

New Zealanders felt that their men had 'won their spurs' (that is, proved their worth) in South Africa. But they had many other reasons, they felt, for being proud of their country. They often said that New Zealand was the most beautiful country in the world. By 1900 they claimed to have the highest standard of living in the world. They were not rich by modern standards. For instance, in 1899 a Taranaki dairy farmer earned about £150 a year (a few thousand dollars in

modern terms). But certainly they had good food and led healthy, outdoor lives. This, too, made the people feel that New Zealand was a good country to live in.

Another thing in which New Zealanders took great pride was their sporting achievements. Their racehorses were making a name for themselves in Australia. In 1883 Martini-Henry won both the Victorian Derby and the Melbourne Cup (in record time) in his first two starts.

A New Zealand tennis player, Anthony Wilding, was one of the best in the world. From 1910 to 1913 he won the men's singles each year at Wimbledon. Several times he and an Australian, Norman Brookes, won the Davis Cup for 'Australasia'. Wilding was killed during the First World War.

There is no doubt that the sport in which the New Zealanders took the greatest interest was rugby football. By the early twentieth century the All Blacks were beginning to have a remarkable number of successes. The most notable were during a tour of Great Britain in 1905. They beat England, Scotland and Ireland, losing only one game, to Wales, out of thirty-two. And they claimed that against Wales they had scored a try that had not been allowed. Altogether they scored 830 points while their opponents scored thirty-nine. There was no doubt that they were among the best rugby players in the world.

The New Zealanders were also very proud of their achievements in politics. The measures passed by the Liberal Government under Richard Seddon had made the country widely known and admired. In France, England and the USA books were written describing New Zealand's new laws, such as old-age pensions. The New Zealanders claimed that their country was 'a working man's paradise', where no one was really poor.

National feeling in New Zealand centred largely on men's affairs — rugby and war. Partly that was because through the nineteenth century there had been far more men than women. For instance, in 1878 there were 231,000 men and only 183,000 women. A shortage of women was common in new settlements. Many men grew up solely in the company of men.

Nevertheless, the role of women in this society dominated by men was not

A lineout during the rugby game New Zealand versus Midland Counties. 1905.

ignored. It was often said that it was their responsibility to be the mothers of the people who would one day become the nation. It was their job to bring up and educate the new nation.

The fact that New Zealand was the first country in the world to give women the vote was a cause for much pride. Women had become a force in politics. Their organisations, like the National Council of Women, made suggestions to the political leaders, for instance, on increasing technical education in primary and secondary schools, some of which were adopted by the government.

Mrs Stella Allen wrote her opinion about the great future of the nation (apparently meaning separate from Australia when she talked of remaining 'isolated'):

> We are a special people, assuredly a little superior to others and destined to guide the world in the path of social reforms. . . . Our destiny is to remain isolated.

A young nation

When people talked about the nation they often talked about children, who were to become the nation. Most people in the colony were young; indeed, in 1878 fifty-two percent of the population was under twenty-one years old. Four people out of every ten were under the age of fifteen. The population was much younger than it is today.

The grown-ups tried to encourage the children to be patriotic citizens. A *School Reader* was published in 1899 to teach the children about New Zealand life, literature and history. The government hoped that it would 'tend to make our children more patriotic and foster love and pride for their country'.

New Zealand ships had flown an ensign showing the Union Jack with four stars (representing the Southern Cross) since 1869. In 1901 Seddon arranged for it to become the New Zealand flag. Flags were given to the schools. In many of them, especially during the Boer War, flag-raising ceremonies were held in the schools. The children saluted the flag and sometimes groups of children marched about doing 'flag-drill'. They also sang patriotic songs such as 'Boys of the Southern Cross'. Thomas Bracken's song, 'God of nations! at thy feet; In the bonds of love we meet . . . ', had been written in 1875 and set to music by an Otago teacher, John J. Woods. It was often sung and was published, for instance, in Bracken's books of poems and in the *Zealandia Song Book* of 1915. In 1940 it was adopted as our national hymn.

There was one way in which the children did invent a national characteristic. Their parents and teachers spoke English like the English or Scots, Welsh or Irish. But the children started to speak their own sort of English; what we would now call the 'New Zealand accent'. By about 1900 almost all New Zealand-born children spoke with what was called a 'colonial twang'. It seems that they taught it to one another at school. ''Old yer 'ead down' they would yell when playing leap-frog. In an early story, *The Bush Boys of New Zealand*, two boys, Dinkums and Mac, escape some boys who are chasing them in the Taranaki bush. 'That was real good-o,' chuckled Dinkums. 'We diddled them properly that time.' The children were using their own slang. Some of it came from Australia. Some they made up for themselves. For example they called a dog a 'guri', which was from the Maori word 'kuri'.

The First World War

Large numbers of New Zealanders fought in the First World War (once called the Great War) from 1914 to 1918. Their first big action began on 25 April 1915 when the Australian and New Zealand Army Corps (the Anzacs) landed at Anzac Cove on the Gallipoli peninsula. Their aim was to fight the Turks and to assist the Royal Navy to break through the narrow Dardanelles Straits and threaten Constantinople, the capital city of Turkey, which was an ally of the main enemy, Germany.

A terrible number of British and Anzac soldiers were killed during the landing, by rifle and artillery fire. The whole campaign was a bad mistake. A big Turkish army occupied the rugged

The summit of Table Top, a steep hill at Gallipoli captured by the Wellington Mounted Rifles on 6 August 1915. This action was part of the battle to capture Chunuk Bair.

heights and the Anzacs were not able to dislodge them. There were terribly heavy casualties on both sides. Both sides fought with incredible heroism in appalling conditions, and none more so than the New Zealanders. They considered that they were the best troops there — tougher, and with more initiative and dash than the British. Some of the observers, generals and journalists said the same thing.

In one famous action in 1915 Colonel W.G. Malone and his Wellington Battalion took the summit of a high hill, Chunuk Bair, and looked down upon the Dardanelles. But they were slaughtered by Turkish rifle and machine-gun fire. Some of them, including Malone, were killed by shells fired by a British warship. Of 800 men who had attacked, only seventy were unwounded when they were relieved by Otago and Wellington men. The Turks retook the heights. Between 6 and 9 August, 1,800 New Zealanders, both Pakeha and Maori, out of the 4,500 men fighting had been killed or wounded. Altogether 2,700 New Zealanders died at Gallipoli, and 4,700 were wounded.

In December 1915 the troops were all evacuated from Gallipoli. The British and French and Anzac allies had been defeated. Yet the Australians and New Zealanders felt that the battle had not been for nothing. Their soldiers had proven themselves as good as the best in the world. A British general said that ancient Greece 'had no more glorious story'. The Anzacs were heroes to be compared with the most famous in history. One New Zealander who fought at Gallipoli later wrote that the struggle on Chunuk Bair was 'New Zealand's finest hour'. It was often said that New Zealand attained nationhood on the bloody slopes of Gallipoli. So a defeat seemed a kind of victory. Ever since, Australia and New Zealand have kept Anzac Day as a day of national mourning in memory of the dead.

The New Zealand Army went on to fight against the Germans in France and Belgium. Before the Germans were beaten nearly 50,000 New Zealanders, over half of those who served on European battlefields, were killed or wounded. That was a very hard price to pay for becoming a nation.

Below left: Sheltering in a huge shell hole.

Below: Burying a dead comrade.

It could not be said that the New Zealanders were a nation by 1918. Many of them were British immigrants who, in some cases, never ceased to be British. But it is true that most New Zealanders had begun to feel that they belonged to a separate nation within the British Empire.

Bottom: On the march through a destroyed village.

FIFTEEN

~

The Years Between the Wars: the 1920s

The First World War ended on 11 November 1918. New Zealanders cele-brated the victory and greeted the thousands of 'returned' soldiers. The thousands who died were not forgotten. Up and down the country war memorials were set up. Sometimes the war memorial by the side of the road is the only sign left that there was once a small township at that place. Many more men were killed in the First World War than in the Second World War. For exam-ple, the district of Drummond, in Southland, sent twenty-seven men to the 1914–18 war. Thirteen were killed. In the 1939–45 war thirty-two men were sent and only five were killed. The First World War had been such a terrible experi-ence that people who lived through it felt lucky to be alive. They wanted to go back to life as it had been before the war.

The 1920s were uncertain years when people's lives were changing very fast but many old ways of thinking persisted. They were not an easy time to live through.

One big farm

The most obvious of the 'old ideas' that people clung to were economic ones. The Liberals had built up New Zealand's wealth by encouraging small farming. Bill Massey, the Prime Minister, liked to think of New Zealand as 'a farm'. Nearly half of our population lived in the country in 1921. Over ninety percent of our exports came from the farms. New Zealand sold wool, frozen meat (mostly lamb), butter and cheese. No other products were very important. The other ten percent of exports came from small amounts of apples, cereals, timber, gold and coal.

Farmers in New Zealand in the 1920s grew grass. On large farms the grass fed sheep and the farmer got his money from wool. On small dairy farms the grass fed cows and the farmer sold milk to a dairy factory, which made butter and cheese. The 'mixed farms' fattened lambs for meat and wool and kept cows as well. Very few farmers raised beef cattle. No one farmed deer. There were few orchards or vineyards. There was little horticulture, except for market gardens.

New forests were planted in the 1920s, but the results were not seen until the 1940s. Farming was enormously important. The whole country depended upon it to earn money overseas. But the range of products was very limited. However, there was one odd kind of farming practised at this time. The Prime Minister was one of many farmers who kept ostriches. He had some on his farm at Mangere. Ostriches were cheap to keep. They would eat almost anything. Their tail feathers were very fashionable for trimming hats and the fluffy ostrich down was used to trim evening dresses. Ostriches are again being farmed but for meat and leather rather than for feathers.

Ostriches on the 'Helvetia' ostrich farm at Pukekohe near Auckland. They are on their way to the plucking shed.

When the soldiers came back from the war there was a rush to settle them on the land. Many found work in towns but 7,000 or more were helped to buy land. Land prices were high and so were prices for wool, meat and butter. The war was over and good times seemed ahead. Almost a million hectares of new land were opened up on soldier settlement schemes. Much of this land was rough and not really suitable for the dairy farms the men were trying to make. Often after the first crop the thin soil was exhausted. The new farmers had paid too much for the land and were heavily in debt. They did not have enough money over for animals, tools and fences. In 1920 prices for farm products suddenly fell; farmers who had borrowed heavily could not keep up their payments and families had to leave their farms. Dairying, the type of farming that had seemed to be the most profitable, was hit the hardest.

The sudden shock of falling prices for butter, meat and wool in the early 1920s did not turn New Zealanders towards different products. The only answer to falling prices seemed to be to produce more. In 1914 we sold 22,000 tonnes of butter. In 1921 we sold 46,000 tonnes and at the end of the 1920s we averaged 76,000 tonnes.

Scientific farming

The spectacular increases in production were managed by using science to help farming. New Zealand was one of the first countries in the world to apply science to farming. In the 1920s the new approach produced some amazing results.

New Zealand soils did not naturally grow the best grass for cows and sheep. Soil scientists looked at soil needs and advised on more suitable grasses and fertilisers. With their help farmers were able to keep their paddocks in 'permanent pasture'. Before this time they had to plough and re-sow their land in new grass every few years. By top-dressing with the right fertilisers, farmers could keep all their land in grass. They could grow extra for hay and ensilage, and no longer needed to grow special feed crops for their animals in winter. The new pastures would feed many more animals.

Science also improved the animals. No new breeds of sheep were developed at this time, but dairy herds were changed dramatically. Cows had been chosen for their looks and the amount of milk they gave. The idea that they could be tested for butterfat production had been around since 1910, but no one had been very interested. After 1922 groups of farmers began to join herd-testing associations. Cows that produced milk with a high butterfat yield were valued. Others were culled. Some breeds, especially Jerseys, were found to be particularly good butterfat producers. By the end of the 1920s Jerseys were the most common breed of cow in dairying areas. In 1929 each cow on a dairy farm produced seventy-two percent more butterfat in a season than her grandmother had delivered in 1901.

The Morrinsville Calf Club meets for its prizegiving in the 1930s. The children have reared a fine group of Jersey calves.

The changes to better grass, more stock and more profitable stock caused changes to the way families ran their farms. Ploughmen and horses were no longer needed. Much more

machinery was invented and used. The most important invention of the 1920s was the milking machine. The first of these were petrol driven, and later electric milking machines were made. They enabled a farmer to milk far more cows than he and his family had been able to milk by hand. The first machines were not perfectly reliable, and when they broke down, as they often did, then the family had to milk all the extra cows. But as the machines grew more efficient they made life easier for farming families.

Electricity had been used mostly for lights. Now it was used to drive machines and heat water. Hot water and electric milking machines in the cowshed were followed by electric light and electric stoves in farmhouses. Telephones and radios reduced isolation for country families. It was rare for every house in a district to have a radio, but people gathered to 'listen in' in homes that did have them. By 1927 there were over 30,000 radios in New Zealand homes.

A transport revolution

A change so great it was almost a revolution in the way New Zealanders lived happened in the 1920s. Motor cars became available. Before the First World War there had been only a few cars in New Zealand, and they had been mostly seen in the towns. Outside the towns roads were rough — dusty and stony in summer and muddy in winter. During the war no cars could be imported but after 1918 they poured in.

Donald Brown was fourteen years old in 1919. He was in the third form at Auckland Grammar School. His father decided to buy a car and the two of them went down to the wharf to see it unloaded. It was a black 1918 Dodge tourer and it came from America fully built up, in a car case. Donald's father, like most adults at that time, never learned to drive. (On his first and only attempt he backed the car through the garage wall!) A special permit was obtained from the local council so Donald could drive his father around. Donald was, in practice, in charge of the Dodge. He loved it so much he used to sit in it after school doing his homework. His friends at school called him 'Dodge' Brown.

In 1924 registration of motor vehicles was made compulsory and the numbers could be counted. In 1930 there were 150,571 cars, 29,870 trucks, 1,269 buses and 36,323 motorbikes registered in New Zealand. Roads had to be built for all these vehicles. Just as people had clamoured for railways in the nineteenth century, so they demanded sealed roads after 1918. Many small towns died because people could drive to bigger towns to do their shopping and business. A petrol tax of fourpence a gallon was introduced in 1927 to raise funds for main highways.

Road accidents became a new problem: 176 people were killed on the roads in 1928. The number of deaths in motor accidents passed the number of deaths by drowning, which had been the most common form of fatal accident.

Cars were a constant temptation. People who owned them drove too fast in them. People who did not own them helped themselves. The new crime of car conversion was invented in 1919. In 1924 the punishment for car conversion was

Round trip to Taupo 1920

In 1920, when Don Brown was fifteen years old, he drove his father and three friends to Taupo. They left Auckland on a Saturday with spare wheels strapped on behind, two spare cases of petrol and the luggage tied on to the running boards. The main road to Hamilton had just been covered with uncrushed metal which had quite big rocks in it. These could do a lot of damage to cars ('I was sick of tying the exhaust pipe back on'), so Don crossed the river and went down the far side. They reached Tirau on the first stage. That was about 200 kilometres.

While they were at Tirau it rained all night and three kilometres beyond the town the metalled road stopped: 'We put on the chains and slid and slithered all the way to the Mamakus.' There were frequent stops to clean out mud jammed in a solid mass under the mudguards. As they climbed the Mamakus the tomahawk came into use to cut ti-tree for the wheels to grip on. An obliging farmer and his horses pulled them some of the way. They spent the next night at the Prince's Gate Hotel in Rotorua.

The stage from Rotorua to Taupo took all the next day: 'I didn't know anyone who'd ever driven to Taupo. No one I knew in Auckland had ever been there.' When they reached Taupo their petrol was used up and there was none at all in the town. They had to wait two days until some more was brought in. On the way back they went over completely unformed roads to see the new hydro station at Atiamuri: 'There was good engineering in those early cars. They had to stand up to conditions that today's cars simply could not survive.'

Don Brown's Dodge ready for the trip to Taupo. A special holder to carry two tyres has been welded on to the back. You can see the loops at the top of the kick plates. These were for tying luggage and cases of petrol safely on to the running board.

increased from £5 to £20. 'It is becoming quite a common thing for young fellows of the "hoodlum" type to take a car and go off for what I understand is called, a "joy-ride",' said a Member of Parliament indignantly. Parliament was still worrying about car conversion in 1927. In 1935 the fine was increased to £200 and the courts were given the power to send offenders to prison. The number of cars, and car thieves, went on growing just the same.

Donald Brown's Dodge was a very good car for that time. It had electric lights, an automatic starter and a vacuum pump system to feed petrol into the engine. Even so, driving any distance in it was a complicated task. Donald had to plan ahead. Tyres were very poor quality until about 1925, so two spares were always carried. There were no petrol stations. Petrol was bought from grocers in four-gallon tins, two to a wooden case. They cost £1 ($2) a case, which was a lot of money in 1919. Donald always carried a spare case of petrol strapped to the car's running board. When he filled the car Donald used to put an old felt hat into the funnel and strain the petrol through it. The felt would keep out any drops of water that had crept into the petrol.

Three motor vehicles outside the Dunlop Rubber Company's offices. The large car is a 1918 Dodge tourer with its hood down just as Don Brown liked to drive his. The truck is an early electric truck. It was powered by banks of batteries under the body and in the morning, on the flat, could manage ten miles an hour. By the end of the day, however, 'it could hardly reach the garage'. The smaller car is an early Morris Cowley with carriage-lamp style lights.

A fifty-kilometre drive from Auckland to Pukekohe on clay roads took four hours. If there was only one stop to change a wheel, that was considered a good trip. In winter, chains would have to be put around the tyres to get the car through the clay. On longer trips a tomahawk was standard equipment for cutting ti-tree from the side of the road to help the wheels grip. About forty kilometres an hour was a good average speed for the Dodge. It could reach up to seventy kilometres per hour, but not for long because the radiator would boil.

Early Model T Fords had no automatic starters and no petrol pumps. Their petrol tank was under the front seats. If the tank was less than three-quarters full and the car was going uphill, petrol would not get through to the engine and the car would stop. To keep petrol running to the engine Model T drivers used to go up hills backwards.

Towns grow suburbs

In 1926 there were nearly one and a half million people in New Zealand; Pakeha and Maori. The movement of people to the North Island was continuing: sixty-two percent lived in the North Island in 1926. In 1926 nearly sixty percent of the population lived in towns. More efficient farming and the use of machines meant that fewer people were needed to run farms. New Zealand depended upon farming to earn almost all of its overseas funds, but more and more of its people were living and working in towns.

Towns and cities began to spread out. Suburbs grew along the main roads and tram lines. Trams and buses took workers between homes and jobs. They no longer needed to live in the same part of town as they worked in. Shops were built where the trams and buses stopped. Sometimes people rushed to buy sections in the new suburbs and then found they could not afford to build houses. Families were living in tents at Point Chevalier in Auckland in 1925, and one couple lived in a shanty made of car cases.

The villa at 30 Bellavista Road, Herne Bay, built for William Brown's family in 1909. It cost £700 (1,400) including the cost of the section and is typical of the style of quality suburban homes at that time.

When they were settled in their new houses children enjoyed 'the steady stream of callers to the back door'. All kinds of household goods were delivered in those days. The butcher, the grocer and the bread man called regularly. At Christmas the Chinese greengrocer gave his best customers porcelain jars of pre-

served ginger instead of calendars. There was a man in Herne Bay who delivered tea. Every few weeks the coal man came to fill up the coal house. Once a week the ice man called. He wore a thick sack over his head and another across his shoulders and brought a big block of ice to put in the ice box. Each block lasted exactly a week.

The 'flicks'

Movie theatres followed people and shops into the suburbs in the 1920s. By now they were not a novelty any more, they were a part of people's lives. The first moving pictures, called 'kinematographs', had been seen in New Zealand in 1896. There was no story, just pictures moving on a screen. They seemed marvellous. Then touring 'picture shows' would travel about the country setting up their equipment in local halls. Some of them showed short films of real events. Queen Victoria's diamond jubilee procession was filmed, and in 1901 huge crowds in New Zealand watched films of the old Queen's funeral. After about 1900 films began to tell stories. Some of these were made in Australia. In 1907 *The Story of the Kelly Gang* was popular in New Zealand.

There were many problems with the early movies. The films flickered. There was no sound and no colour. The projectors made a lot of noise — whirrs and clicks — as the film went through. The film was highly inflammable and often caught fire. This could be dangerous because the projector was usually in the middle of the crowd when films were shown in halls. The first buildings made specially for movies were built in the cities in the 1910s. Auckland's first, the King's, opened in 1910. The new picture theatres were a great improvement on halls. The noisy projector was put in a special fireproof box at the back.

By the 1920s movies were very popular. Auckland alone had twenty-five picture theatres. Hollywood was making quite long films and 'film stars' had appeared. The first cartoon was made in 1915. Some movies were made in New Zealand. Rudall Hayward made *Rewi's Last Stand* in 1925. Saturday afternoon sessions, showing lots of cartoons and serials like Buffalo Bill, Hopalong Cassidy, Tarzan and Flash Gordon, became a regular weekend pleasure for suburban children in the 1920s and 1930s. Many of their parents booked regular Saturday night seats at the local picture theatre and went along every week.

Most films shown in the early picture theatres were black and white. But colour was invented before sound. The first 'talkie' was a collection of Movietone

Movie programmes and advertising from the 1920s. Film audiences liked to buy souvenir programmes for films, just as they did for stage shows.

News shorts, shown in the Paramount Theatre in Wellington on 8 March 1929. Queues to get in to hear 'the marvel of the age' stretched all the way down Courtenay Place and along Cambridge Terrace. The grandest picture theatre in New Zealand, Auckland's Civic, opened on 18 December 1929 with a talkie, *Three Live Ghosts*. The Civic cost £205,000 to build and had 3,500 seats.

Electric lights and electric household gadgets, motor cars, telephones, radios and movies seemed to make life more exciting in the 1920s. Aeroplanes were another challenge. The first flight across Cook Strait was in 1920. The Tasman Sea was more difficult. It was not until 1928, after several fliers had been lost, that Charles Kingsford Smith flew the Tasman in his plane 'The Southern Cross'. It took him fourteen hours twenty-five minutes. Thirty thousand people went out to Wigram to see his plane come in, and thousands more shared the occasion by listening in on the radio.

Trouble on the horizon

Part of the mood of the 1920s was optimistic. Machinery was making life easier for some people. Inventions and gadgets were making it more exciting — 'It was a marvellous time to live in if you were keen on machinery.' But underneath all the progress there were worries and problems. The 'progress' of the 1920s had a shallow base. Many New Zealanders were worse off than they had been before the war.

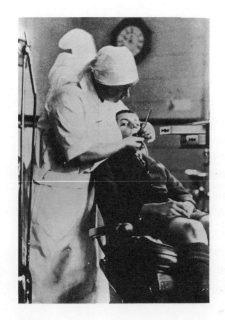

The dental nurse at Beresford Street school dental clinic at work. This photo was taken in 1927.

Prices for the goods we needed to sell overseas had been high in 1919 and 1920, then had fallen suddenly in the next year. They wobbled upwards a little way and then slid down again. It was rather like the end of the 1860s, when the wars and gold rushes had been followed by depression. The Government's answer in the 1920s was like Vogel's in the 1870s. They borrowed to bring back the good times. Most of the borrowed money was used to help farmers. Massey, who was Prime Minister from 1912 to 1925, and Gordon Coates, who led the Government from 1925 to 1928, were North Island farmers. They saw the answer to New Zealand's problems as helping farmers to produce more butter, meat and wool.

For many families, especially in towns, the 1920s was a hard time. Low prices for farm products affected businesses in the towns. Many people were out of work. Health, especially that of children, was affected by poverty. Food prices kept going up. Housing was expensive, rents rose, and families crowded into cheap old houses and boarding houses in the run-down old parts of the cities. They caught diseases such as tuberculosis and diphtheria and passed them on. They could not afford doctors or medicine. School medical checks

showed that most New Zealand children had bad teeth and many also had eye, ear and skin diseases. Dr Elizabeth Gunn, the first director of school health, reported that many children 'were absolutely blocked up with infected tonsils and adenoids'.

Toothbrush drill at the King George V Memorial Health Camp at Otaki.

School medical checks also showed that one New Zealand child in every ten did not get enough to eat. Hungry and badly fed children grew up with crooked legs because of a disease called rickets. Iodine deficiency caused goitre. In 1925 Wanganui schools gave children who were seriously under weight half a pint of milk and a biscuit a day, and allowed them twenty minutes' rest instead of physical education.

Health camps were started in 1919 to look after such children. At the same time the School Dental Service began to train dental nurses. The first dental nurses began work in 1923. By 1931 there were 203 clinics; enough to look after about half the children in New Zealand.

The plight of families, and especially children, was bad enough for the first family allowances to be paid in 1926. The allowances were very small — mothers could get two shillings (20 cents) a week for every child in the family after the first two. They were paid only to poor families whose income was less than £4 ($8) a week. They were not paid to 'foreigners', nor to families where either parent was 'of bad character'. They were not paid to unmarried parents. Probably the Government thought that hardly any mothers would need the allowances. They got a shock. By 1930 allowances were being paid to 3,868 families.

At the end of the 1920s it was clear that they had been years of uneasiness as well as progress. The hopes of a better life after the war had not always been met. In the election of 1928 the aged 'financial wizard', Sir Joseph Ward, promised to borrow £70 million ($140 million) 'for the use of the people'. The people were delighted by the idea and Sir Joseph's party won the election. The 1920s began with good times arising out of the end of the war. They ended with exciting promises of borrowed millions. Neither state of mind had a solid foundation.

SIXTEEN

❧

The 1930s: Depression and the Welfare State

The shaky economy of the 1920s grew worse, not better, in the early 1930s. Sir Joseph Ward could not borrow the promised millions. In July 1930 he died, leaving behind him a government with hardly any ideas about how to cope with the rising numbers of jobless New Zealanders.

There had been 6,000 people out of work at the end of 1929. A year later there were 11,000. Slowly the government began to organise job programmes. The first programmes depended upon local councils and private employers finding work to be done. Government would then help to pay the wages. The number of men out of work rose higher and higher; the first schemes could not cope. In February 1931 Scheme 5 was announced. For many people it came to represent all that was wrong with New Zealand during the Depression.

Work programmes

Scheme 5 followed the pattern of earlier programmes. What was different about it was its size. There were so many jobless men and boys that it was impossible to find worthwhile work for them all to do. Councils had to invent work and supply any materials needed. Naturally they looked for ideas that cost as little as possible. Gardening and chipping weeds at the roadside were common projects because they were cheap. Building new roads or drainage schemes cost more for tools and materials. Nevertheless some were undertaken, usually with the most primitive tools so that the work would cost less and last longer. Shovels and wheelbarrows were used on road projects instead of bulldozers. Irrigation canals were dug with spades. Men working on these jobs knew they were not being used efficiently. The pay, which came from the government, was meagre. Single men were paid fifteen shillings ($1.50) a week and married men were paid more, according to the number of children they had. The highest pay, £2 ($4) a week, was for married men with three or more children.

Some Scheme 5 projects were useful, although even these were carried out slowly so as to make the work last. School playing fields were built, such as those at Mount Albert Grammar School and Wellington College. Tourist roads

Workmen during the Depression. 1932.

like Auckland's Scenic Drive and the road to Milford Sound via the Homer Tunnel were Scheme 5 projects. So was the great Ngauranga Gorge entrance to Wellington. Many thousands of hectares of pine trees were planted in forestry projects.

The worst unemployment was in 1932 and 1933. The exact numbers are not known, but the official figures reached 81,000 in 1933. These statistics do not include the thousands of people, mostly women and teenage boys and girls, who were working on farms and in domestic work. Such workers were housed and fed but seldom earned more than a few shillings a week above their keep.

Food riots

Rage at the meanness of the relief schemes overflowed into rioting in 1932. On 9 January of that year a crowd of unemployed, many of them women shouting 'We want food,' smashed the windows of Wardell's grocery shop in Dunedin. In April the government cut wages for state employees and also reduced pensions. On 14 April a protest meeting was held at the Auckland Town Hall and in the evening a crowd outside the hall tore palings off the fence around the

167

Mounted police charge into a protest meeting of unemployed in Cuba Street, Wellington, in 1932. Except for one man who broke his leg scrambling over a fence, no one was seriously hurt.

Methodist Mission at the bottom of Airedale Street and ran down Queen Street breaking shop windows. About 250 shops were broken into. A fruit-shop owner saved his windows by quickly putting cases of fruit outside his shop and asking people to help themselves. They did, and moved on. The *Auckland Star* reported that many of the broken windows had small round holes in them, caused by boys shooting marbles from catapults. The next night windows were broken in Karangahape Road. A force of 2,000 police, army, navy and volunteers was organised to keep order over the weekend and Auckland quietened down. On 10 May shop windows were smashed in Wellington after a march on Parliament.

The 1932 incidents were riots, not revolution. The Forbes Government pushed a law through Parliament called the Public Safety Conservation Act, which gave it enormous emergency powers in case of further riots. Some improvements were made to Scheme 5, pay was increased a little. The people waited for the next election.

The 1935 election was fought on the question of living standards. Everyone agreed that New Zealanders should have jobs and decent homes, but they did not agree about how to achieve that goal. We depended upon prices paid overseas for our farm production. Prices had begun to turn around in New Zealand's favour in

1934. The Coalition Government of Forbes and Coates kept on spending as little as possible and relying on better overseas prices to improve New Zealand conditions. To some extent this was happening. Unemployment was only about 50,000 by the end of 1935. But living standards, especially for the unemployed, the unskilled, young people, women and Maori, had fallen to very low levels.

Life in the Depression

This letter, written to Walter Nash, MP for Hutt, shows how one poor family lived in the 1930s. The family consisted of a mother and fourteen-year-old daughter, who lived on the girl's tiny wage of £1 ($2) a week.

Dear Sir

You will perhaps remember me calling on you some time before Christmas, and also sending some vegetables to where I was then living. . .

Mr Campbell, of the Charitable Aid in Petone, got my girlie into the Wellington Tobacco Factory. This is her third week and she draws one pound per week. She is not a strong girl by any means, and she is what is called a general and has to work exceedingly hard, and this week she has such a dreadful cold she can hardly breathe, but she would not stay home, as she would lose four shillings per day.

Mr Nash, her money is all we have coming in, and she won't be fifteen till next June. My girlie is a hero; there is not one other kiddie in New Zealand doing what she is to-day, and all she wants on Saturdays is sixpence for the pictures. . .

We have no table, a chair, two boxes, and have our meals off a bench, and till four weeks ago we were sleeping on the floor. Thanks to Mr Roy, of the Smith Family, we were given a bed. We had a mattress and plenty of bed linen.

I wish you could see the place that I am paying rent for. The window is smashed in one room, we cannot use the fireplace, as the rain pours down the chimney and I do not know if any repairs will be done. . .

At the time of the 1935 election there were still thousands of people on Scheme 5. Families were living in dreadful shacks in town and country. Children were not getting enough to eat. The strangest makeshift items were used for clothing. Sacks could be turned into raincapes by cutting them open down one side. They were also used to make boys' pants.

Women made aprons and towels out of flour sacks. Old woollen jerseys were carefully unpicked and knitted up again using the good bits of wool. Pieces of cardboard were put inside shoes when the soles wore out. One woman remembered, 'It was a great day when grandfather died. I inherited all his underwear and I made a whole lot of warm woollen singlets for the children out of it.' By 1935 families had suffered enough to want to vote for a change.

'Micky' Savage

Change was promised by a very ordinary man. He was an Australian who came to New Zealand when he was young. He did not seem especially clever but he always seemed to talk common sense. He understood the hopes and needs of average people. His name was Michael Joseph Savage — 'Joe' to his friends, but the people who voted for him called him 'Micky'. Savage became leader of the Labour Party at the end of 1933. For the next two years he went up and down New Zealand talking about jobs and houses and schools and hospitals. He persuaded people that he understood their needs, and would do something to help.

Labour said that it would not wait for rising overseas prices to bring new life to the New Zealand economy. Its policies were designed to speed up economic recovery. Conservatives said that this meant too much government interference. There is no doubt that people worried about sudden change. They had rejected Labour in 1928 and 1931, even though the economy had been bad then. By 1935 they were fed up with conservative caution — and they trusted Micky Savage. With his gentle smile and his funny habit of starting all important sentences with 'Now then . . .', Savage led Labour to a sweeping victory in 1935.

Above: Micky Savage in a crowd of supporters in 1938.

The 1930s was still the time of the passenger train. All important journeys were made by train. In 1930 Sir Joseph Ward's funeral procession had gone from Wellington to the Bluff by steamer and train, stopping many times for speeches. When Micky Savage went down to Wellington on the train to become Prime Minister it was a triumphal procession. A large crowd, including the Ponsonby Boys' Band, saw him off at the Auckland station and crowds gathered wherever the train stopped. Savage would make a little speech, the crowd sang 'For He's a Jolly Good Fellow', and then cheered until the train was out of sight. He arrived in Wellington to the blasts of train whistles and a welcoming crowd of several thousand, who followed him from the station to Parliament Buildings.

The Prime Minister, Micky Savage, and the Minister of Works, Bob Semple, helping to move furniture into the first state house in Miramar in 1937. Facing the camera on the left of the picture is John A. Lee, the Under-Secretary for Housing. Mr and Mrs McGregor, the first tenants of the house, lived in it for over forty years.

The Labour Government

The main achievement of Savage's government was to improve the lives of ordinary families. They did this so completely that New Zealanders changed their ideas about what an average level of comfort and security should be.

Housing was an especially important area for change. Houses had always been expensive. Families who could not afford to buy houses rented them. Poorer families rented rooms. In bad times people lived in sheds and crowded into shared houses. In Seddon's time the Liberals had started to build houses for workers' families, but only a few hundred were built before the plan was dropped. A few government houses were built for soldiers after the First World War. These early housing programmes recognised that there was a need for the government to build cheap houses, but they were soon abandoned because there was not enough money to meet the need. It was understood that poor families could never own their own homes. That idea was overturned by the first Labour Government.

In 1936 a new Department of Housing was set up. Walter Nash, the Minister of Finance, promised £5 million for houses, and land was found for the first projects at Orakei in Auckland and at Lower Hutt. The first fifty-two state houses were built at Miramar in Wellington. Between 1937 and 1949 the government built an average of 2,475 houses every year. It also lent money through the State Advances Corporation for people to build their own houses.

The state houses of the 1930s were solid, squarish, well-built cottages. Usually they were designed to face the sun, even if that meant turning the house around on the section so that

State Advances Corporation

A corporation set up by the government in 1936 to lend money to people for houses or farms. The Liberals started the system of loans to farmers. The first Labour Government made loans available for housing as well. Later there were two separate organisations: the Housing Corporation for houses and the Rural Bank for farm loans.

A group of state houses in a Wellington suburb.

the living-room did not face the street. That change was considered quite odd. Now we normally build houses to catch the sun.

The new houses were on large sections so that families could grow their own vegetables. They had plenty of cupboards, and built-in wardrobes, which most small houses of the 1920s had not had. Laundries were part of the house and not a wash house in a backyard shed. These early state houses set a new standard for workers' homes.

Housing schemes were continued after 1949 by the first National Government and by all governments since then. Housing became an important part of the 'welfare state'. It was important to family life and it was also important for jobs. New houses created work not only for the men who built them, but for the people who made the things that went into them.

A new lifestyle

As the economy improved in the later 1930s life grew much more comfortable. Wooden and linoleum floors were covered by carpet squares, or even with the new fitted carpets. Radios, refrigerators, electric stoves and water heaters went into the new houses. A few daring women bought electric cake mixers and washing machines. Single armchairs were replaced by matching 'three-piece suites' in the new living rooms. 'Time payment' was invented so that people could buy expensive goods more easily. Farmers department store in Auckland advertised a special 'Magic Brain' radio at 4s 9d (49 cents) a week for two years, and the very latest in boys' bikes, with both front and back brakes, for five shillings (50 cents) deposit and 1s 11d (20 cents) a week for ninety-five weeks. Telephones and motor cars became much more common.

As well as homes, people needed jobs. Much bigger public works projects were started, using men and machinery efficiently. Many of these projects were badly needed. Hydroelectric stations had to be built quickly to generate the electricity that people were eager to use.

One of the new flying boats arriving at Mechanics Bay from the USA in the 1940s.

The desire for better roads kept on growing, along with the number of motor cars. Flying, at first a sport, was becoming a means of transport. Aerodromes were built. Commercial airways linked the major cities by 1939, and regular flying-boat services from Auckland to Sydney began in 1940.

Work was shared out by more subtle methods than the rationing of the early thirties. Pensions were improved so that older people were more willing to retire at the age of sixty. Secondary education was opened to all children up to the age of fifteen, and younger people were encouraged to stay at school. Wages were fixed at a level which was considered enough to keep a man, his wife, and three children. The working week was set at forty hours. The aim was more jobs, at better wages. It still took a long time to get everyone back to work. Scheme 5 was not abandoned until 1939.

There were important changes in health care in the 1930s. Until 1939 anyone who went to hospital was expected to pay for it. Public hospitals cost less than private hospitals, but they were still expensive. There were fewer than a thousand doctors in New Zealand and most poor families could not afford to go to them. People dosed themselves with medicines they bought at the chemist or made up recipes at home. Some of these homemade cures may have been quite dangerous, others were nasty but harmless; some were useful. Aunt Daisy's *Radio Cookery Book* had this recipe:

> *Chapped hands, cracked lips, face sore from cold.*
> *Cut fat from mutton chops, render down in saucepan, leave to set, stir in slowly, enough glycerine to make mixture sticky, mix well. Keep in jar. Apply at night, wipe off with cotton-wool next morning.*

Social Security

After 1935 the leaders of the Labour Government began to talk about 'social security'. They meant that even if people lost their jobs, or fell sick, or became too old to work, they should still be able to live decently. The 'social security scheme', as it was called, took some years to work out and it was very expensive. Without the steadily improving prices for the goods we were selling overseas the scheme could not have been started. Walter Nash, the Minister of Finance, worked out that with the economic conditions improving, and with a special social security tax, the programme could go ahead.

Public health nurses inoculating school children against diphtheria in Christchurch in 1942. Diphtheria was once dreaded by parents because it was a major killer of children. It is now a rare disease thanks to inoculation.

Micky Savage announced the basic points about social security to a packed meeting at the Wellington Town Hall on 2 April 1938. His speech was broadcast and thousands of families listened to him on the radio. He promised better pensions for widows, the disabled, and old people. There would be an old-age pension of £1 10s ($3) a week at age sixty for people who needed it and 'universal' superannuation at age sixty-five for everyone. Savage's audience cheered and stamped and climbed on to their chairs to applaud when he announced these. The second part of the scheme was health care. There would be no charge for medical care, public hospital treatment, medicine, or maternity care. Families had always worried about the cost of treatment for sickness as well as about the illness itself. Now the fear of expense would be taken away.

The social security scheme won Labour an enormous vote in the 1938 election. Free medicines and free hospital care began at once, but the government and the doctors could not agree on free medical care. Most doctors charged about 10s 6d ($1) a visit. In 1941 it was agreed that the government would pay 7s 6d (75 cents) and the doctors would charge the rest to their patients. Many doctors were content with the government contribution and did not charge their patients extra.

The health care system set up in 1939 gave New Zealanders an almost free system for over twenty years. But with time and improved medical knowledge, it began to cost more and more. The amount the government paid doctors became less important than the amount the patient paid. By the 1960s public hospital waiting lists were so long that medical insurance schemes grew up to help people pay for private hospitals. Public hospitals still care for the seriously ill and those who cannot pay for private care. However, a growing demand for health services has led to greater private responsibility for paying for them.

The school system

The educational changes of the first Labour Government have lasted longer than the health reforms. In order to understand what happened we need to go back and look at education as it was before 1935.

Children of Kutarere School near Opotiki in 1912 wear their best clothes for their school photograph.

From the time when settlers first began bringing their families to New Zealand they had worried about education for their children. The 1877 Education Act promised free, compulsory primary education. But for most people in the nineteenth century 'education' meant much less than it does now. They wanted their children to be able to read and write and do basic arithmetic. Most children achieved that in a few years and left school. Primary education lasted from primer one to standard six (now form two). Each class ended with an examination and no one went on to the next class without passing. Clever children could sometimes pass more than one examination in a year. Those who passed the exams for all of the six standards were given a 'certificate of proficiency'. Children who went through primary school quickly could get their proficiency at twelve and go to work. Many children, however, left school before they ever reached standard six. In the 1880s only three percent of children stayed as long as standard four.

No one could go to secondary school without the proficiency certificate. Also, secondary schools were not free. They charged fees of about £10 ($20) a year. Some granted scholarships or 'free places' to bright pupils.

There were only twenty-five secondary schools in New Zealand in 1900. They taught 2,800 students (1,800 boys and 1,000 girls). The biggest was Auckland Grammar School with 344 pupils (both boys and girls). Most secondary schools taught only Latin, foreign languages (usually French) and mathematics. The larger schools taught some science, but only the biggest had science laboratories. The

Gordon Burt photographed these children at a Wellington primary school in the 1940s. The new technology has arrived – the girl in front is using a slide projector.

others taught science from textbooks, without experiments. Some practical subjects, such as woodwork for boys and cooking for girls, were started about 1902, but the pattern of secondary education did not change much in the early twentieth century. It was a narrow kind of education, meant to prepare a very small number of students for university study. In 1920 only thirteen percent of students went to secondary schools and many of those stayed less than a year.

The Depression of the 1930s was a bad time for education. Two of the four training colleges for teachers were closed. The school starting age was put up from five to six. Class sizes of forty or more were quite common. Teachers were put out of work. There was no money for school libraries. Cooking, woodwork and science classes were reduced to save money on materials. Teaching aids meant blackboards and white chalk. Even coloured chalk was an extravagance.

One of Micky Savage's promises was better education and more of it. Peter Fraser, the new Minister of Education, promised 'secondary education for all'. In 1936 proficiency was abolished. Anyone who wanted to could go on to secondary school. Education was free until a student was fourteen. After that a 'free place' was allowed to anyone who earned it by passing examinations. In 1944 the leaving age was raised to fifteen and soon afterwards fees for secondary education were removed. By 1939, sixty-five percent of pupils went to secondary school. Peter Fraser said, 'Continued education is no longer a special privilege for the well-to-do or the academically able, but a right to be claimed by all who want it to the fullest extent that the state can provide.' By the end of the 1940s ninety-seven percent of New Zealand children were going to secondary school.

More schools had to be built and the style of teaching had to be changed to suit a different kind of high school student. Much more money was spent after 1938 on libraries, handwork and art materials, and especially science. Careers teachers were appointed. Intermediate schools were built to help prepare pupils for high school. In 1944 the School Certificate examination was offered so that students who did not want to go to university would have a separate examination to work for. Secondary schools began to teach art and music. There was much more physical education. New subjects such as social studies, biology, commercial subjects, geography and technical drawing were taught.

People argued about the 'New Education' of the 1940s. Some thought that the new subjects, and the move away from teaching Latin and other languages, would make students lazy. They liked the old system, in which secondary

schools taught a few subjects to a small number of students.

Secondary education for all has been an important change to New Zealand life. Nearly everyone goes to school from five to sixteen, and many stay longer. New subjects are taught and schools try to give students interesting experiences beyond the

The New Education: 'Simon Says' in a primer classroom at Island Bay School in 1949.

classroom. Teaching is more than blackboards and chalk. Films, video equipment and computers are everywhere. In many schools the students log into the Internet. Many of these changes began in the 1930s and 1940s.

By the end of the 1930s the ordinary family in New Zealand had seen real change in the kind of life it could expect to have. Thousands of new houses had been built. Jobs and pensions had made incomes more secure. The sick could expect to be looked after. Education had been much improved. These changes more or less add up to what we call 'the welfare state'. An active and imaginative government after 1935 helped to make the welfare state. But the changes would not have been possible without the good prices which our exports earned in the late 1930s, 1940s and 1950s.

Students now use the Internet as well as library books. These Lynfield College pupils are downloading information.

177

SEVENTEEN

Wars and the Fear of War Since 1939

In the twentieth century the world has been torn apart by wars between the great powers and their allies. These wars were fought to conquer or to defend large parts of the earth. In the years 1914 to 1918 Great Britain, France, Russia, the United States, and their allies, including New Zealand, fought to prevent the expansion of Germany and its allies, including Turkey.

General Freyberg.

In the 1920s the Italians set up a dictatorship under the Fascists and in the 1930s the Germans came under the rule of Nazis. In the years 1939 to 1945 there was another world-wide war, as the democracies — Great Britain, France, the United States and their Communist ally, the Soviet Union — fought to save the world from the Nazis. New Zealand fought alongside the democracies.

A New Zealand division fought heroically in the deserts of North Africa against the Germans and Italians. The division also fought, unsuccessfully, to save Greece and Crete from the conquering Germans. They were driven out by the German Army, but not before inflicting heavy losses on the enemy. At Maleme airport in Crete New Zealand troops killed large numbers of crack German paratroopers before being forced to withdraw. The Germans lost about 4,000 men in the fighting in Crete, and they never used paratroopers in that sort of fight again.

The New Zealand division was led by Major-General Bernard Freyberg, who had won the Distinguished Service Order (DSO) at Gallipoli and the Victoria Cross (VC) in France. After the war he was to become the first New Zealander to be Governor-General.

By mid-1943 the British 8th Army, including the New Zealanders and the Americans, who joined in the war at the end of 1941, had beaten the Germans and Italians in North Africa. The New Zealand soldiers then joined in the battle for Italy, fighting their way up that long country. They took part in some major battles, including that at Cassino, where a famous abbey had been built, cen-

New Zealand troops chatting in a Cretan village, 1941.

turies before, on top of a hill. This was occupied by the Germans, who could observe every approach.

Cassino was attacked by an army of British, Indians and New Zealanders. The monastery was bombed, which later led to much criticism of General Freyberg. The ruins provided excellent defensive positions. Two companies of Maori troops managed to occupy the Cassino railway station, but tanks were unable to get across to defend them. The bombing had made the area almost impassable. When the Germans counter-attacked with tanks the surviving Maori had to withdraw.

The battle continued for two months. The German paratroopers fought as bravely as the British, Indians and New Zealanders. In the end the Allies pulled out their forces and by-passed Monte Cassino. Later most of the Germans left and it was taken by Polish troops.

More than 17,000 Maori fought in this war, many of them in the famous Maori Battalion. One of them, Te Moananui-a-Kiwa Ngarimu, earned the Victoria Cross, the highest award for bravery.

On 7 December 1941 the Japanese joined in the war on the side of the Germans. They bombed the American naval base at Pearl Harbor and rapidly conquered Malaysia, French Indo-China, and the Dutch East Indies and other places. For the first time New Zealand was threatened by attack from an enemy. As the Japanese pushed south they invaded New Guinea. They bombed Darwin in Australia and sent midget submarines to attack shipping in Sydney Harbour. The Japanese were beaten in some big naval battles by the United States Navy. Thousands of American marines and soldiers came to New Zealand. Fortunately the country was spared from attack.

In 1945 the Germans and Italians were beaten. Russian, American and British armies reconquered Europe. The Japanese gave in after the Americans dropped the first atom bombs on Hiroshima and Nagasaki, where many thousands of people were killed.

Left: New Zealand troops blacking their faces before attacking Green Island.

Below: Troops practising landing on the coast.

New Zealanders fought in the Air Force, for instance as fighter pilots in the Battle of Britain, and in the Navy as well as in the Army, all over the world. Some fought in the Pacific Islands against the Japanese invaders. There were many casualties — 11,600 dead and 15,700 wounded — but the losses were not as severe as those during the First World War. Several hundred thousand people served in the armed forces. In 1942, for instance, there were 154,500 in the forces, including 8,500 women in the women's services, the WRENS (the Women's Royal Enlisted Naval Service), the WAAF (the Women's Auxiliary Air Force) and the WAAC (the Women's Auxiliary Army Corps).

The war took over the lives of the women and children almost as much as the men. Most families knew men away in the armed forces, whether fathers, brothers, sons or friends. Everyone longed and prayed for their safe return.

The war at home

Every grown-up had to help with the war effort. Men and women without children, who were not in the forces, were 'manpowered' to work in essential industries, that is, industries essential for winning the war. Large numbers of 'land girls' worked as farm hands. University students — most of whom were girls, except in medicine, science and engineering — all worked in key industries during their vacations.

Many women and old men helped with fund-raising for the war effort. Women helped by sewing and knitting clothing for the servicemen. They baked fruit-cakes (which keep for a long time) and packed up food parcels to send to the servicemen overseas. Small children, especially in Auckland, helped to collect ergot, a sticky fungus growing on grass, which was used to make a substance that helped to stop bleeding. They also helped with house-to-house collections of scrap metal, bottles, paper and anything else that might help the war effort. Children also helped at 'bring and buy' stalls to raise money for the war.

At school, children practised air-raid drills — what to do if they were bombed. In public parks, and often at school or in their back yards, trenches were dug and covered to serve as air-raid shelters. Many schools issued 'survival kits' to the children. Some of these included simple cotton-gauze gas

Devonport air raid practice.

masks. Some included a cork on a string. If bombs went off you bit the cork. It was supposed to stop you from biting your tongue!

During the early part of the war there were often 'blackouts', when no sign of light was allowed to be visible outside the buildings. Blankets or other covers were put on all windows.

Many things could not be bought in the shops, because they could not be imported. Petrol, meat and other foods were rationed. You had to take ration coupons to the butchers and the garages.

Every day people talked about the war — the invasion of Europe, the first atom bomb dropped on Japan. The newspapers were full of war news. One day a little girl in Auckland went home from school and her mother said, 'The war is over!' The girl asked, 'Won't there be any more newspapers now?'

Cold War

A war between Russia and the USA, fought with words and threats, not with the armed forces, broke out between the Communists in Russia and the United States with its allies, including Great Britain. The democracies accused the Communists of seeking to rule the world. The Russians feared attack by the United States with its atom bombs. In 1949 the Chinese Communists took over their own country, the most populous country on earth.

New Zealand and Australia became allies of the United States, which had saved them from the Japanese. In 1951 they signed the ANZUS treaty of friendship, to help one another if attacked.

Sometimes the 'Cold War' became hot, as fighting broke out between Communists and non-Communists. Several times the New Zealand armed forces were in action in wars not as widespread as the two world wars. In the early

1950s they went to war when Communist North Korea invaded South Korea. They later fought against Communists in Malaya. In the mid-1960s small New Zealand forces were sent to help the Americans to fight the Communists of North Vietnam (and

Part of a protest against the Vietnam War.

some Vietnamese who were not Communists, but just wanted the Americans and other foreigners to leave their country).

For the first time in New Zealand many people opposed sending troops to a war. As in the United States, thousands of citizens, especially young people, demonstrated against the Vietnam war. They thought it wrong for New Zealanders to be fighting there and felt that the Vietnamese should be allowed to decide on their own form of government. In the end, in 1972–73, the Americans and their allies pulled out of Vietnam. They had lost the war.

One reason why so many people opposed the war in Vietnam was the fear of a bigger one; the fear that it might spread to include the other great powers, especially Russia. They feared that if there were another 'great war' it would become a nuclear war.

People were also frightened of nuclear explosions. The great powers, and former great powers like France and Great Britain, were often testing nuclear weapons. They liked to do this far away from home. The French began to test their weapons on a Pacific island, Mururoa. New Zealanders asked why, if these bombs were as safe as the French said, they did not test them near Paris. In 1972 some small ships from New Zealand sailed into the test zone near Mururoa to protest. The following year Norman Kirk, the Labour Prime Minister, ordered two New Zealand frigates, *Otago* and *Canterbury,* to steam near Mururoa during further French tests. This protest received world-wide publicity. It

Hundreds of people made up this nuclear-free symbol in a protest outside the Auckland War Memorial Museum.

expressed the fears of most people about nuclear weapons and war. New Zealand was seen as making a strong, independent statement in opposition to nuclear weapons.

In the past both Pakeha and Maori had seen fighting as a source of fame and honour for brave men. But now the great powers and some other countries had nuclear weapons and rockets to deliver them. A world war could mean the death of most of the people on earth. In other words, war, on a large scale, was too dangerous to wage.

In 1987 the Lange government passed legislation which prohibited nuclear-armed or nuclear-powered warships in our coastal waters.

184

A protest march against nuclear-armed and nuclear-powered warships in New Zealand waters.

EIGHTEEN

Modern Times

The life of the Maori changed enormously when the Europeans came. The lives of the European farmers changed very much at other times, such as after the invention of refrigerated shipping in the 1880s. But it is debatable whether the lives of most New Zealanders have ever changed as rapidly as since 1945, the end of the Second World War. This chapter will describe how the life about us, what we do and see every day, in different parts of the country, has changed. The main change has been that more people became well-to-do and fewer people were poor.

The Labour Government had been led by a Scot, Peter Fraser, after Micky Savage died in 1940. He was a hard-working war-time leader and a clever man, but he did not have Savage's warm personality.

The first National Government

During the war industries shut down because of bombing in many countries. Many factories changed over to making materials of war; tanks, for instance, instead of motor cars. As a result many goods could not be bought. Food was rationed; sugar and eggs were hard to get, cream and chocolate disappeared from the shops. During the war people accepted this. But afterwards they blamed the government. They called it 'the shortage government'. In the 1949 election Labour was beaten by the National Party, led by Sidney Holland, a Canterbury businessman. He promised to 'make the pound go further'.

After the war there were many strikes and other troubles in industries, especially on the wharves. Many workers wanted more pay: they had had hardly any pay rises since the war began. Sid Holland decided that the unions should be taught a lesson: that he was boss. In 1951 the 'wharfies' went on strike (although they said that the bosses had locked them out). There was a long strike, lasting over three months. Most of the unions opposed the strike, and eventually the wharfies gave in. The government broke up their union into a number of small ones. After this there was peace in industry for some years.

From the end of the 1940s until about the late 1960s New Zealand was one of the wealthiest countries in the world. Only the Americans and Canadians, and sometimes the people in one or two European countries like Sweden, were better off. In these years the world was eager to buy our meat, butter and wool and paid good prices for them.

Demand for wool during the Korean War pushed wool prices to record levels.

Wool reached 240d a pound (equivalent of 600 cents a kilo) in 1951. It was so valuable that some farmers paid children to go round with sacks collecting tufts of wool from their barbed-wire fences.

A time of prosperity

There is no doubt that most people found that they had a better living standard, and that they owned more things than earlier generations. And there is no doubt that they enjoyed the new lifestyle. During the Depression up to 1935 many people could not afford to buy what they wanted. Then, during the war, goods had been short.

Sidney Holland.

When, in 1957, Sid Holland listed the achievements of his government, it was a long list of 'goodies' that had increased under National: 'People had more money, pensions, sheep, cattle, telephones, motor vehicles, houses, electric toasters, vacuum cleaners, washing machines, radios, overseas trips, university scholarships and aircraft for aerial top-dressing.' The rabbit menace, he said, however, had declined. 'New Zealand,' the Prime Minister wrote — and with every justification, 'is a happier, healthier and more prosperous nation.'

The fact was that before the Second World War very few homes had refrigerators or washing machines. There were still some districts which had no electricity. In 1937 there were, in the whole country, only 250,000 radios — or, at least, that number of radio licences had been issued. By 1981 sixty-seven percent of houses had colour television and thirty-four percent had black and white television. Some houses had both. Radios were no longer licensed and no one knew how many there were. By 1995, New Zealanders watched, on average, two hours and forty-two minutes of television each day.

The Goldsbury children, John, Pat and Robin, and their parents admire the family's first car, purchased in 1954. It's a new Austin A40.

A family watching television. 1962.

In 1937 there were 211,000 cars, trucks, taxis and motorcycles in the country. That was one vehicle for every seven of the 1.5 million people. By 1981 there were 1,700,000 motor vehicles of all sorts owned by a population of 3 million people; more than one vehicle for every two people in New Zealand. By 1996, there were 2,487,722 vehicles registered, while the population had only increased to 3.5 million.

In 1967 a system of decimal coinage replaced pounds, shillings and pence with cents and dollars. The new dollar was the equivalent of ten of the old shillings.

The good years continued under Prime Minister Keith Holyoake and then, in 1967–68, there was a sharp shock. Overseas prices for our products suddenly dropped. Unemployment reappeared for the first time since the war and quickly reached 7,000. Many businessmen went bankrupt — that is, they lost all their money. The 1968 hiccup was scarcely over before the world inflation that followed the Vietnam War struck New Zealand. There was a sudden increase in inflation in 1970–71, a slight fall in 1972, and then from 1973 through into the 1980s high inflation continued. Since 1976 New Zealand's inflation rate has run ahead of that of our trading partners. This made it very difficult for our primary producers to get an economic price for their goods. From 1974 New Zealand's exports did not earn enough to pay for our imports and for ten years governments borrowed to maintain a high standard of living.

A changing society

During the long years of good times, say 1949 to 1973, very many changes could be seen in New Zealand life, often as a result of the development of new machinery.

Some jobs have almost disappeared as a result of the increasing use of machinery. For instance, before the Second World War most farmers used to make

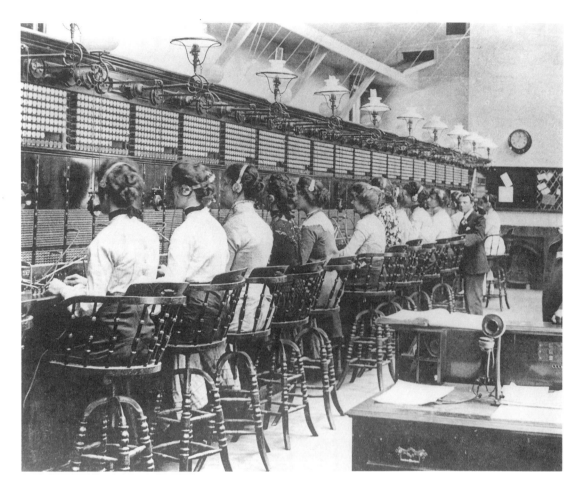

haystacks. The hay was raised in a 'grab', which was on a line pulled, usually, by a horse. The 'crow', often a boy, stood on top of the stack and forked the hay to the 'stacker', who built the stack. Now machines bale or roll up the hay instead.

Young women telephonists at work at the Auckland Central Telephone Exchange in 1903, closely supervised by the manager.

The early telephones were all run from manual exchanges operated by large switchboards. Thousands of girls and young women worked as telephone operators. Then automatic exchanges were introduced. Many of those telephonists then became typists or Burroughs adding machine operators. Now they run word processors or computers. Fashion also leads to jobs changing. Until the 1950s all adults and most girls wore hats when they went out. Hundreds of milliners and machinists were needed to make the hats. Then hats went out of style and the art of millinery nearly died out.

Many new industries, some very big, have been started. These include a steel industry, making iron and steel from local iron-sands. A glass works was started at Whangarei. Large hydro-electricity projects produced power for the nation and for new industries, including an aluminium smelter at Bluff. Another important new industry produced pulp, paper and particle board from huge pine and other forests, planted in the 1920s and later. Technology has transformed the ways ports operate and ships are loaded. New Zealand is now much more

Clothing industry workers at lunch, c 1900.

industrialised than it was in the 1930s. As a result of these changes there are more workers employed in factories than on farms or in mines. Many people, such as public servants, teachers, shop assistants, truck drivers and bank clerks, have jobs in 'service' industries. They do not make things but provide useful services. The total workforce in 1981 was 1,325,000 people.

Primary industries (agriculture, forestry etc.)	11.2%
Secondary industries	23.2%
Services	62%

By contrast, in 1901 the proportions were:

Agriculture	74.5%
Industries	13.1%
Services	11%

There has been an even bigger change in many homes. In 1936 less than four percent of married women went to work. In 1981 thirty-five percent did so. Altogether 310,000 married women worked full time or part time. Of all the workers, over one-third were women and girls. Before the 1950s most of these women would have worked at housework and contributed to their family's standard of living by the quality of their sewing, baking, fruit preserving and jam-making. Beautiful smocked party dresses and fine baby knitting was all done at home. Another change has been that in many homes there is only one parent, a solo mother or father. Home life, and so the lives of children, have changed greatly because of these changes in working habits and in families.

Going to work has been only one change in women's lives. In most occupations girls and women were paid less than men who were doing the same job. It was argued, by men, that men had to feed families and women did not. In recent years it became clear that this was unfair. 'Equal pay for equal work' has been introduced since the 1960s. Women have fought to be treated as well as men, which was not always true in the past. 'Women's lib' — the women's movement to get equality — has had a big influence on our lives. Changes in the law have meant that everyone in New Zealand now has equal access to jobs, housing, education, public facilities, goods and services, whatever their race or ethnic origin, their sex, their marital status or their religious beliefs.

There has been another, perhaps equally big, change. Before the Second World War very few Maori lived in the cities. For instance, in 1936 there were only 1,700 in Auckland, the biggest city. During and after the war there was a huge heke (migration) to the cities. By 1945 twenty percent of Maori lived in towns; by 1976 seventy-six percent of Maori did so. Their work contributed enormously to the country's growing industries and its increasing wealth.

There were other new groups of workers. Some were European

Women workers packing sausages at AffCo in Auckland.

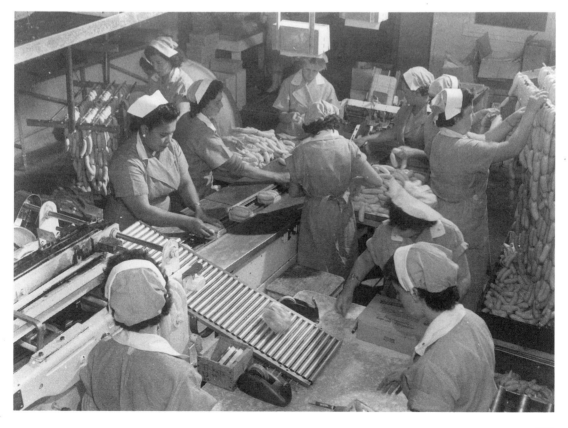

Manager and workers at a Christmas party at an Auckland factory, gathered round a suckling pig. It is an Auckland Polynesian feast.

immigrants, Dutch and British. By 1991 there were 123,000 Pacific Islanders living in New Zealand. They came from Western Samoa, Tonga, the Cook Islands, Niue and other Pacific Islands. There were more Polynesians in Auckland than in any town in the Pacific. Maori and Pacific Islanders make up about thirteen and a half percent of the population. Asian immigration accounts for another two percent.

In the past, in the towns and cities, most Pakeha New Zealanders had not met many Maori or Asian people. Peoples with different ways of life — Pakeha and Maori, Cook Islanders, Tongans, Chinese and Cambodians — now had to get to know one another. They had to 'get on'. This was one result of one of the biggest changes of all in New Zealand in modern times, the growth of the cities. The goods we export still mainly come from the country: meat, wool, butter, cheese, timber. But eighty-five percent of the people now live in cities; or, rather, in suburbs or towns.

Population					
	1913	1951	1981	1991	1996
Auckland	217,000	329,000	769,000	885,500	1,068,645
Christchurch	143,000	207,000	321,000	307,000	309,028
Wellington & Hutt	127,000	174,000	321,000	326,000	357,648
Dunedin	86,000	95,000	114,000	109,500	118,143

Facing new problems

Since about 1972 New Zealand, like many other countries, has had difficult times. In 1956 we had the highest income per person in the world. In the 1980s we slipped to about seventeenth. This was mainly caused by the rapid rise in the price of oil and petrol. The price went up four times in 1973 within a few months. New Zealand's exports did not earn enough money to pay for oil and our other imports. Once again there were people out of work.

Sir Robert Muldoon,
Prime Minister 1975–84.

Many New Zealanders migrated across the Tasman to find work in Australia. Yet most people did not give up hope, as many seemed to do during the Depression of the 1930s. In those days many people hoped that Great Britain, the 'motherland', would help them. Now New Zealanders knew that they had to fix up things themselves. In the 1970s and early 1980s, very big natural gas and other 'energy' projects were started to make the country more independent in fuel and power. New marketing strategies were developed for our primary produce.

The main economic strategy between 1975 and 1984 was to borrow from overseas to maintain New Zealanders' comfortable lifestyles and to hope for a return of good times. Many people trusted the Prime Minister and Minister of Finance, Sir Robert Muldoon, to protect them from the economic realities of a changing world. Under Muldoon, government debt rose ($10 billion was borrowed to pay for fuel and

David Lange,
Prime Minister 1984–1989.

power projects called Think Big) and unemployment steadily increased. Inflation was 16% at the end of 1975 and touched 20% in 1982. Muldoon wielded enormous powers of personal control over prices, wages, interest rates and many other parts of the economy. He introduced what was called a wage price freeze. But New Zealand could not hide forever from the economic forces overseas. We had to trade and interact with other countries to survive. In July 1984 Muldoon lost an election and David Lange became Prime Minister with Roger Douglas as Minister of Finance.

The new government began a programme of sweeping economic reform that lasted from 1984 to 1992. The system of government control of the economy, slowly built up since 1935 and especially since 1975, was swept away. All kinds of regulations and taboos were abolished. Some of these affected our lifestyles

Roger Douglas, Minister of Finance 1984–1988.

Below: Ruth Richardson and Bill Birch.

as well as the economy. The government no longer controlled the exchange rate; Saturday shopping was extended and Sunday shopping permitted; radio stations were allowed to broadcast on FM after 1984.

Roger Douglas asked basic questions about what governments were for. Was it necessary for the state to own forests and run airlines and railways and telephone systems? In the nineteenth century it had been necessary for the state to start these things because no private person had enough capital. Douglas asked if the state was still the best manager of these businesses and decided it wasn't. Many things the government owned (and taxpayers had had to find capital to maintain or improve) were sold. Government funding was cut and the number of government workers was reduced from 88,000 in 1985 to 34,500 in 1995. Jobs outside the government and in the private sector eventually rose after a period of high unemployment. The Reserve Bank Act 1989 made it an essential part of the bank's job to control inflation. In 1991, a National Government continued the reforms under Ruth Richardson, the Minister of Finance, and Bill Birch, the Minister of Labour. Compulsory unionism was ended and changes were made to the welfare system.

After almost ten years of economic restructuring, government debt fell and there was a steady rise in the number of jobs. New Zealand is said to be among the most competitive countries in the world. In the new 'global economy' a small trading country like New Zealand needs to be efficient and competitive to survive.

The House of Representatives.

MMP

The changes of the eighties made many people very unhappy. The restructuring of the economy had left many unemployed or worse off. Many people were forced to change their employment or move to other towns where employment might be available. They felt that their views were not represented in Parliament. Two parties — Labour and National — seemed to dominate politics and many thought that politicians could not be trusted. There was a great deal of discussion about changing the way Members of Parliament were elected, in the hope of getting a more representative system and improving the accountability of politicians.

A referendum in 1992 indicated that about 55 percent of the electorate wanted to consider change. A second referendum in 1993 demonstrated a preference for the mixed member electoral system over the traditional first past the post system. The 1996 general election was the first to be held under the MMP (Mixed Member Proportional) electoral system. Each voter had two

MMP: The new system

The main characteristics of the MMP system are:

- **65** rather than 99 **electorate Members of Parliament,** made up of 5 Maori seats and 60 general seats.

- Each registered party can have a **party list** of candidates, with their most favoured ones early on the list. Each party can decide whether or not to include electoral candidates on their lists.

- **55 new party list seats** will be created to top up electoral seats for each party in such a way that:

  each party's share of MPs in Parliament will reflect its share of the party vote.

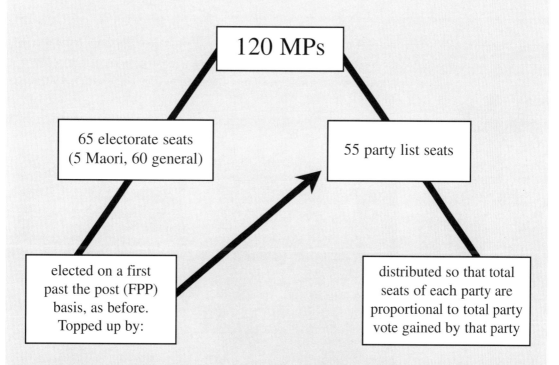

However a party will have to win at least five percent of all the party votes or at least one electorate seat in order to be allowed to get any party list seats. This is called the **threshold.**

Above: Janet Frame wrote her autobiography in three volumes: To the Is-land, An Angel at my Table and The Envoy from Mirror City.

Below: James K. Baxter is widely regarded as the most gifted poet New Zealand has produced. He died in 1972, aged 46.

votes: a party vote to choose what party they wanted to represent them in Parliament, and an electoral vote to choose their electorate member. A large number of parties contested the election. In the new parliament there were more women than ever before, the first Asian MP and increased Maori representation. After a prolonged period of negotiation a Coalition government was formed, from the National Party with Jim Bolger as Prime Minister, and from the New Zealand First Party with Winston Peters as Deputy Prime Minister and Treasurer.

It could be argued that New Zealanders are more confident than in the past that they are a nation. They are proud of their achievements, especially of their great athletes like Yvette Williams, Peter Snell, John Walker and Danyon Loader; and of the success of national rugby, cricket and netball teams in recent years. But they are also proud of the work of their famous writers, like the poet James K. Baxter; the novelists Janet Frame, Sylvia Ashton-Warner, Maurice Gee and Witi Ihimaera; and the short-story writers Katherine Mansfield and Frank Sargeson. Margaret Mahy is one of the best writers of children's stories in the world. The work of painters like Frances Hodgkins and Colin MacCahon has also helped to make New Zealanders proud of their country and their people. They feel that their nation will have a great future; that it has the natural resources and talented people on which to build that future.

Right: Margaret Mahy has written more than one hundred books and won many awards.

Far right: Witi Ihimaera was a career diplomat before becoming a full time writer.

Top: Beatrice Faumuina won a gold medal for her discus throw at the 1997 World Track & Field Champs in Athens.

Above: Sir Edmund Hillary was the first man to climb Mt Everest. He reached the summit with sherpa Tenzing Norgay on 29 May 1953.

Left: Jonah Lomu, renowned for his speed, agility and size, is regarded as one of the best rugby players in the world.

NINETEEN

The Changing World of Children

The nineteenth and twentieth centuries have been times of amazing leaps in technology. Maori came to New Zealand in great sailing canoes, and the Pakeha settlers in sailing ships. Basically they were the same form of transport. Now it is possible to fly the Atlantic on supersonic passenger planes, send goods across the world in nuclear-powered container ships navigated by computers and surf the Internet.

It is not surprising, then, that the lives lived by each generation of New Zealand children have been quite different. The amount of work children are expected to do, the age at which most of them start work, the clothes they wear, and the families and homes they live in have all altered so much that a child born in, say, 1870, would have had a very different life from one born in 1910 or 1980. Changes have happened just as quickly in the ways children amuse themselves and how they spend their free time.

Westport children dressed up as nursery rhyme characters for a fancy dress party. The boy is the Knave of Hearts and the girl is Little Bo-Peep.

Victorian children

In the early days of settlement, as we have seen, children's work was so necessary to the family's survival that they probably did not have much time to themselves. When they did have time to play, it was easy to escape from the supervision of busy adults. Games could be rowdier and dirtier, and much rougher, than would be allowed in suburban neighbourhoods now. Exploring, fishing, bird-nesting and sailing home-made rafts on creeks and rivers were all common pastimes. Hide-and-seek on the edges of the real bush or in a 'clearing' after a burn-off could be really exciting and sometimes dangerous. Huge logs made a natural adventure playground. The book called *The Bush Boys of New Zealand,* written by a New Zealander about Taranaki, describes such a place:

It was a typical 'log-clearing', but the latter term is misleading, in regard to such a place. The 'bush' had indeed been 'felled', and the

fire sent through it, burning up the scrub and branches and small wood, but great charred logs and stumps still covered the ground so thickly, lying one across another in all directions, or piled in great heaps, that, at little distances, scarce a patch of bare earth was visible.

Ward McAllister took this rather prim photo of a Sunday School picnic at Wanganui in 1910.

   It seemed a vast sea of logs and trunks of trees, which, tumbled about in inextricable confusion, formed apparently a totally impassable labyrinth.

Groups of children sometimes gathered for chasing and battle games. Chasing games like 'Cowboys and Indians', 'Pakehas and Maoris', or 'Boers and British' were great fun in the bush. In the 1870s stories of the Ned Kelly gang in Australia made 'bushrangers' the favourite game of New Zealand boys. There was plenty of rough ground for battles. These could last for a number of days, but when boys used real weapons, like heavy sticks, leather belts with buckles and shanghais or catapults, people were seriously hurt. Adults would then have to put a stop to the games.

   Even in the 1890s, when towns had become quite settled, battles were a regular kind of amusement. Boys of all ages joined in. There was a battle in Collingwood on Guy Fawkes Day in 1895:

   Guy Fawkes Day was a battle royal. Different parts of the village clashed together with flax whips and rotten eggs. Later all would combine to burn the guy.

Children of all ages played singing games and tagging games. 'Oranges and Lemons' and 'Farmer in the Dell', which are now small children's party games, were played by children of up to thirteen or fourteen. Parlour games like Lucy

Locket, postman's knock, musical chairs or pass-the-parcel were also played by all ages; but these were inside games and there were not very many houses with enough room to play them in. The cluttered Victorian parlours filled with ornaments and little tables were hardly suitable for games.

When church halls were built Sunday Schools became a wonderful source of Sunday afternoon entertainment. There were book prizes for attendance and picture cards to collect or use as hymn-book markers. Sunday School picnics were looked forward to for weeks. So were the 'tea meetings', where sandwiches, cakes and lemonade were followed by games. These brought indoor games into the lives of many more children. Dressing up as the title of a book, or acting out book titles was very popular. They played charades and word games as well as parlour games. 'There was always a noticeable improvement in attendance in the week or two before a tea meeting.'

School games

When education was made compulsory in 1877 schools were places where children met regularly. School playgrounds were strictly divided into boys' and girls' areas. Children organised their own play and there was little supervision. The girls' playground was usually smaller than the boys', and their games were quieter, with less room to move. Singing games, cat's cradle and knucklebones were girls' games; so were swinging and skipping. Skipping rhymes lasted for generations. Here is one that was used in the 1890s, but is probably much older:

> *Dancing Dolly had no sense*
> *She bought some eggs for eighteen pence*
> *The eggs went bad*
> *And she went mad, 1, 2, 3, . . .*

Cockfighting in the boys' playground at an Auckland school in 1927.

Collections were very popular. Pressed flowers and birds' eggs were collected and swapped. Pictures from magazines and poems were pasted or copied into albums. Boys, too, collected birds' eggs, stamps and cigarette cards. Boys' playground games were adapted from the games they played outside school. Piggyback fighting was a favourite and so was 'kingy-seeny'.

Kingy-seeny had been played from quite early times. Two sides would agree on a 'kinging ground' and build forts, one on each side. A big boy in the centre of the ground was 'he'. The others would then take turns to run across the ground and the boy that was 'he' had to catch them. When someone was caught he was held down on the ground and 'kinged' by chanting a rhyme with his name in it and patting him three times on the head:

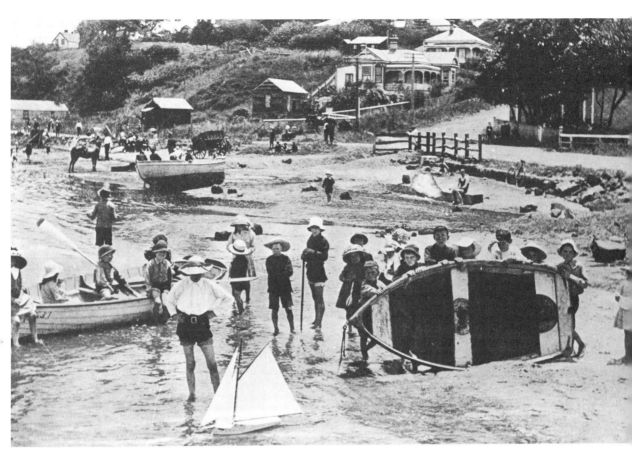

Kingy-seeny, one, two, three
You're the very man for me
Keep him quiet, hold him down
Pat him thrice upon his crown
Blackball, Blackball, one, two, three
Jimmy Roberts, you are 'he'.

Children playing on
Onehunga beach in the
Christmas holidays, 1913.
Most of them are wearing
sunhats and have taken off
their shoes, but there are
plenty of long sleeves.

If the victim could escape during the kinging he had to be caught again. Any kind of resistance, including biting, was allowed. As the number of 'kings' increased it became more dangerous for the runners and the game ended with the kings storming the forts. Children play a version of this game called 'bullrush' in school playgrounds by having their teams behind lines at each end of the playground.

Sports needed more organisation than games and children did not play them very much before 1900. The most popular sports in settler society were linked with work. There were chopping and ploughing competitions and shooting matches. Horse racing quickly became popular with Maori as well as Pakeha. The first recorded race was in Wellington in 1841, and 3,000 people went to races in Auckland in 1842.

Because sea and river transport was so important in the early days, everyone was interested in showing off their skill in a boat. Auckland's first races on the Waitemata Harbour were held in 1840. Rowing races as well as sailing races were

203

Changes in the style of beach wear are very obvious in these pictures taken between 1914 and 1946. In the formal photo of Ola Clarke and her mother on Devonport beach in 1914 the baby is in her best bonnet and Mrs Clarke wears a veil, long gloves and a hat trimmed with birds. The cheerful picture of Jack Petrie at Motutapu in 1919 and the girls at Mairangi Bay in 1946 show that the attraction of sand and water is the same at all times. Children were pleased when tickly woollen bathing suits were replaced with fast-drying nylon suits.

organised and the whale boats were the stars of the show. Rowing shells specially made for rowing as a sport were not invented until the 1860s and 1870s.

Adults played rugby and cricket. Children played 'shinty', or rounders, with bats made from the heavy green stems of big flax plants or pieces of wood roughly shaped with tomahawks. Balls were usually made by rolling up a pair of socks really tight and sewing them into shape. A harder ball could be made by whittling a suitable piece of woody fungus with a pocket knife. Footballs were made by stuffing meal bags with rags and sewing them up: 'They were good balls but they hurt your toes.'

The early 1900s

After 1900 teachers spent more time supervising playgrounds and organising games. The roughest games were banned; running and chasing games began to give way to more recognisable sports. Girls began to be included in rounders and softball; they also played basketball and netball.

Bigger children stopped playing the old children's games and turned to sport when it became available to them. By the 1920s home-made gear was disappearing, except for younger children who still made bows and arrows and catapults. Balls bought in shops were used by everyone. Softball gloves and football boots were rare, however, and no one except serious athletes had running shoes.

Some children had really beautiful toys. There were dolls' houses specially made by cabinet-makers, and dolls with porcelain faces, real hair and glass eyes. They had layers of frilly petticoats, kid gloves, and buttoned boots from France or Italy. Most children had rag dolls or knitted gollywogs. Teddy bears were invented in America in the early 1900s. They were named after President Theodore ('Teddy') Roosevelt. Tops and kites were often home-made. So were stilts and hobbyhorses. Sets of knucklebones were 'cadged' from friendly butchers, but some resourceful children searched farmers' paddocks until they found a rotted sheep carcase and collected the bones themselves. Old knucklebones became polished with use, some were dyed different colours. A good set was a prized possession. So was a big bag of marbles. Marbles was played by men as late as the 1870s, but for adults it was usually a gambling game. Boys and girls played it for skill and playground mana.

Marbles had a whole language and ritual of its own. The target marbles, according to their type, were 'dakers', 'dubs', 'dukes', 'glassies', or 'changers'. The thrown marble was a 'taw' or a 'shooter'. There were many different kinds of marbles and their value changed according to fashion. Many of them came from bottles, where they were used as stoppers. A Wellington boy remembered:

> When I first went to school, bottlies were good currency, being classed as two-ers, but usually soda-waters and black-bottlies counted as the equivalent of six-ers. Rapidly this changed and first of all, bottlies were classed as two-ers and then two-ers were not acceptable as currency. There was just nothing you could do with them

These boys were photographed around 1910 playing marbles on a patch of rough ground.

except use them in shanghais [catapults], a practice much discouraged by adults, especially those with windows on to a street.

By the 1920s, toys bought in shops were replacing home-made toys in the same way that organised games were taking over from made-up games. Knucklebones disappeared almost completely from playgrounds until plastic sets were imported in 1954 and the craze came back for a time.

Children's amusements had always changed with the seasons. Games came and went according to mysterious timetables, which no adult really understood. March was the time for marbles. The first day of winter was the day skipping ropes had to be taken to school. Hopscotch was a game for early mornings in winter. 'Tiggy' and 'hidey-go-seek' were played all year round.

The latest craze

The twentieth-century revolution in communications made local patterns into widespread crazes. Railways, roads and telephones drew the separate parts of New Zealand together into one society. Children shared in this oneness. Movies and magazines brought instant images of overseas fashions. If kewpie dolls or Meccano sets were what overseas children had, New Zealand mothers bought them for their children, too. The first chocolate-covered ice creams, called 'Eskimo Pies', entranced children in the 1930s. American soldiers here during the

Second World War introduced wonders like bubblegum, double-decker sandwiches and hamburgers.

Advertising had almost ignored children until the 1950s. When advertisements did mention children it was to sell necessary things like highchairs, clothes or cough mixture to their parents. From the 1950s advertisements began to feature toys and games. Everyone wanted a walkie-talkie doll or a Monopoly set.

At about the same time, in the 1950s, a teenage culture began to develop. Teenagers and older children wore a distinctive style of clothes. Some of them deliberately adopted clothing styles that shocked adults, and formed into tribes that called themselves strange names: 'milk-bar cowboys', 'bodgies and widgies' or 'punks'. They also developed their own music.

Music, except for songs, had been very much a group pastime. As we have seen, an amazing number of New Zealand children learned to play the piano. People gathered in each other's homes or in halls to make music and amuse one another. A typical entertainment took place in Invercargill in 1896: the cantata 'Esther' was performed with an orchestra consisting of Mrs Wood (piano), Mr Mayo (first violin), Mr Goold (second violin), Mr Ferguson (double bass), Mr W. Ferguson (viola) and Mr Wills (cornet). Refreshments were served in the interval. For other audiences there were bands who played in park bandstands at weekends. No public celebration was complete without two or three bands. In 1910–11 J.P. Sousa's band came to New Zealand and drew huge crowds.

Without performers there could be no music. Technology changed all this. Recording machines meant that people could

This carefully posed picture of the McAllister family as a musical group was taken in 1912.

listen to music played at another time and place. Gramophones were being sold in the 1890s and the first radio broadcasts were heard in Wellington and Auckland in 1922. By the 1930s many homes had them. Popular songs could be heard all over the country, indeed all over the world, at the same time. Singers who had never left Los Angeles or London were heard in New Zealand's living rooms. Frank Sinatra and Bing Crosby were idolised in the 1940s.

Pop stars

ANNA PAVLOVA

GRAND OPERA HOUSE
Wellington
Direction · J. C. WILLIAMSON LTD.
Season Commencing SATURDAY, 12th JUNE.

The programme for Anna Pavlova's tour in 1926 shows the ballerina in her most famous role — the swan.

The first wave of these 'pop' (popular) singers sang for adults. Children listened (some, like Judy Garland, Shirley Temple and Deanna Durbin, became stars themselves), but children did not choose the music. Radios were solid, expensive pieces of furniture, plugged into the living-room wall. Parents, usually fathers, controlled the knobs. Portable record-players and transistor radios changed all that. From the 1950s and 1960s older children and teenagers could tune in to their own music. Bill Haley and his Comets brought in rock-and-roll music in the middle of the 1950s. Elvis Presley's big hit, 'Heartbreak Hotel', was made in 1956, and his first movie, *Love Me Tender*, the same year. Teenagers all over the world struggled into tight jeans and slicked their hair back with Brylcreme into ducktail haircuts. Clive Petrie, aged six, went off to the barber without his mother and came home with a crewcut.

A surprising number of performing stars visited New Zealand. Anna Pavlova danced here (and we called a dessert after her). Laurence Olivier and Vivien Leigh came here with the Old Vic Theatre Company. Dame Nellie Melba sang. So did New Zealand's own opera stars: Oscar Natzka, Inia Te Wiata, and later, Donald McIntyre and Kiri Te Kanawa. Percy Grainger, the composer of 'Country Gardens', toured in the 1920s and again in 1935. Virtuoso musicians like Paderewski, Arthur Rubinstein and Yehudi and Hephzibah Menuhin played here. Igor Stravinsky conducted concerts of his own music in 1961. But all these came to perform for adult audiences.

In the 1960s a completely new kind of artist arrived — the pop star who came specially for teenage audiences. Johnny Devlin was the first. He caused scenes of hysteria only surpassed when the Beatles arrived in June 1964.

Crowds of fans followed the Beatles' every movement. Children stayed away from school to try to catch a glimpse of them. Twenty truant officers were on duty in Queen Street in Auckland on the afternoon of the Town Hall welcome. Fans clambered up the fire escapes of the Beatles' hotel trying to get inside: 'We could hear footsteps all over the place.' The Beatles have been followed by a steady stream of pop stars. Michael Jackson's concert in 1996 was very popular. Fifty years ago there was nothing like them, they are creations of our own time.

Public entertainment

In Maori society and in nineteenth-century settler society amusements were public events. The tribe or the township got together to organise important occasions. Group celebration gave drama and interest to ordinary people's lives. Sporting competitions and picnics sometimes drew huge numbers of people. Ten thousand went down to Bluff on special trains for the New Year's Day regatta in 1898. At that time the town of Bluff itself contained only 1,300 people. Almost any public event became an excuse for people to get together to sing a few songs, listen to the bands and make speeches. The Prime Minister or the Governor-General passing through a little town would be an excuse for a half-holiday from school, a parade, and some kind of public gathering.

Election meetings were highly entertaining. Speakers were expected to be able

Kiri Te Kanawa is a world-famous soprano. She has performed many times in New Zealand.

to deal amusingly with hecklers and to shout down the opposition. Seddon's nickname was 'Old Leather Lungs', because of the deafening bellow he could produce on the platform. When Harry Atkinson toured the South Island in 1884 his Christchurch meeting ended in an uproar, when fighting broke out between the speaker and members of the audience. Political banquets where, apart from the food, the main entertainment was songs and speeches, drew hundreds of people. The speeches lasted for hours.

Opposite: Charles Haines drew this poster to advertise the Centennial Exhibition of 1939–40.

Many community gatherings celebrated progress of some kind: the opening of a school or post office, the christening of a new harbour board tug, the opening of a road or bridge. As the two ends of the Main Trunk railway crept slowly towards each other through the middle of the North Island each new station was opened with a separate celebration.

The most elaborate celebrations of progress were exhibitions. The exhibition craze began with the great Crystal Palace Exhibition organised by Prince Albert in London in 1851. Exhibitions were meant to be celebrations of industry and progress, but displays of curiosities crept into them as well, and funfairs and sideshow alleys sidled up alongside the educational displays. The Victorians loved them. Faint traces of them linger on still in the form of trade fairs and events like Auckland's Easter Show.

New Zealand sent displays to overseas exhibitions from 1862 to 1897. They included Maori cloaks and carvings, gold, flax, and wood samples, and cases and cases of stuffed birds. We also held ten exhibitions of our own, beginning with the Dunedin Exhibition in 1865 and ending with the Centennial Exhibition in Wellington in 1940. The most popular was the Christchurch Exhibition of 1906–07. New pavilions and a complete Maori pa were built for the occasion. Attractions included Fijian firewalkers, a baby show with 300 entrants and a brass band contest. The sideshow alley had a water chute 18 metres high. Nearly two million people passed through the turnstiles in the six months it was open.

Selwyn Toogood's radio show 'It's in the Bag' was one of the attractions of the Auckland Easter Show in 1954. The giveaways on stage are the very latest washing machines and refrigerators. To add to the excitement the show was filmed for experimental television.

The grandest exhibition was the one put on for New Zealand's centennial. It opened on 8 November 1939. It used what was then very advanced technology to amuse and at the same time to educate people about New Zealand's achievements. In the Dominion Court visitors could walk around a huge model of New Zealand. Trains ran up and down the Main Trunk line, city lights clicked on and off, inter-island ferries glided across Cook Strait, and model steamers chuffed in and out of the major ports. Twenty-seven government departments organised displays in the Government Court. The Post Office showed off its new teleprinters. There were live broadcasting studios (radio was less than twenty years old). There was a walk-through model of the Waitomo Caves, with glow-worms that switched off if there was too much noise. The Health Department produced a talking robot called 'Doctor Well-and-Strong'. 'Playland', the amusement park, had an ice ballet, a fat lady who said she weighed 340 kilograms, a roller coaster, a ghost train, and a giant slide. Two and a half million people visited the Exhibition before it closed on 6 May 1940.

The Centennial Exhibition marked a turning point in public entertainment. In its nature it looked back to the Victorian era, but its technology pointed to the future and to completely different kinds of amusement.

Even small children are now familiar with multimedia systems in their own homes.

Home entertainment

In recent times smaller families and roomier houses have given families private places to spend their time. Instead of people going outside their homes for amusement, once the radio was installed, amusement came in to them. The early radio programmes were much like having neighbours in for a visit. The most popular personalities took cosy names: 'Uncle Tom', 'Aunt Daisy', and 'Uncle Scrim'. The hours of broadcasting were filled by hordes of ordinary folk who came to perform for the fun of it. Children were especially enthusiastic. Music teachers took their pupils 'to play on the radio'. Aunt Daisy began her career by producing a children's song show for 2YA called 'The Cheerful Chirpers'. Uncle Tom's Friendly Road Children's Choir performed every Sunday night for years. A quiz show featuring children called 'The Quiz Kids' began in 1948 and lasted nearly twenty years. Selwyn Toogood began the give-away programme 'It's in the Bag' on radio in the early 1950s. Radio news and commentaries (sports broadcasts began at the end of the 1920s) gave thousands of New Zealanders a chance to share in major events. But the sharing was done from inside their separate houses, not by gathering in public places.

Television was introduced to New Zealand in 1960. It was black and white and broadcast three times a week. By 1968 seventy-five percent of New Zealand homes had a set. Home-based entertainment became even more popular. The big movie theatres of the 1930s and 1940s were no longer needed, and many suburban picture theatres closed. The audience for evening radio dropped away. But with the introduction of FM radio and talk-back shows, radio remains popular. And despite dire warnings that television would ruin social life, people continued to talk to one another and read books. Transistors, walkmans and the video revolution made amusement still more individual. Each person can choose his or her own programme. Personal computers have individualised games in the same way.

Technological change in our lifetimes has allowed us to control our own private worlds in ways which our ancestors could scarcely have imagined.

INDEX

Illustrations

The authors are very grateful to librarians in the Alexander Turnbull Library, the Auckland Public Library, the Canterbury Public Library, and the Auckland War Memorial Museum for their very great assistance in finding the illustrations for this book. The following numbers refer to the pages on which the illustrations appear.

Alexander Turnbull Library; 13, 17, 19 upper, 21, 23, 24, 27, 28 upper and lower, 29, 30 lower, 33, 35 upper, 36, 37, 38, 40 upper and lower, 43, 44, 46, 47, 50, 54, 58, 60 lower, 61, 62, 65, 68, 69, 70, 71, 72 upper, 79 lower, 82, 83 upper and lower, 85, 87, 88, 91, 94, 95, 96, 103, 105 upper and lower, 108, 109, 125, 126, 127, 128, 129, 130, 131, 132 upper and lower, 133, 134, 136 upper and lower, 137, 138 upper and lower, 139, 141, 142 upper, 143 lower, 149 upper and lower, 152, 153 lower, 157, 158, 160, 161, 163 upper and lower, 165, 167, 168, 170, 171, 172, 174, 176, 177 upper, 178, 179, 180 upper and lower, 181 upper, 182, 187 upper, 195, 198 upper and middle left, 201, 206, 207, 208, 210

Auckland Public Library; 31, 35 lower, 39, 49, 52, 56, 60 upper, 66, 67 all pictures, 93, 104, 107, 122

Auckland War Memorial Museum; 8, 18, 20, 22, 25, 26, 30 upper, 32, 63 upper, 64, 74, 77 upper, 80, 99, 100, 101, 106, 111 upper and lower, 114, 115 upper and lower, 118, 123, 151, 153 upper, 154, 164, 175, 181 lower, 189, 190, 191, 202, 203

Australian War Memorial, Canberra; 155 all pictures

Authors' collections, 97, 98 upper, 110, 112 upper right, 120, 162, 177 lower, 200, 204 all pictures

Bay of Plenty Times; 144 upper and lower left

Canterbury Museum; 63 lower

Canterbury Public Library; 48, 73, 75, 77 lower, 84, 89, 90, 98 lower, 116, 150

General Assembly Library; 79 upper

Hocken Library, Dunedin; 59, 72

Kokiri Paetae; 145 upper and lower left

Leopold, Vicki, 198 lower right

Leue, Holger; 145 lower right, 209

National Art Gallery; 19 lower

New Zealand Herald; 142 lower, 143 upper, 173, 183, 184, 185, 188, 192, 193 lower, 194 lower, 196 upper right, 199 lower left and right, 211

New Zealand Picture Library; 199 upper

Philips Electronic; 212

Surridge, Jonette; 6

Taranaki Museum; 81

Tauranga Museum; 112 upper left and lower

Te Papa Tongarewa Museum of New Zealand; 11, 14

TVNZ; 198 lower left

Webb, Murray; 196 upper left

Whakatane Beacon; 144 middle